A Long Short War

The Postponed
Liberation of Iraq

Christopher Hitchens

A PLUME BOOK

A
Slate
BOOK

PLUME
Published by the Penguin Group
Penguin Group (USA) Inc., 375 Hudson Street,
New York, New York 10014, U.S.A.
Penguin Books Ltd, 80 Strand, London WC2R 0RL, England
Penguin Books Australia Ltd, 250 Camberwell Road,
Camberwell, Victoria 3124, Australia
Penguin Books Canada Ltd, 10 Alcorn Avenue,
Toronto, Ontario, Canada M4V 3B2
Penguin Books India (P) Ltd, 11 Community Centre, Panchsheel Park,
New Delhi—110 017, India
Penguin Books (N.Z.) Ltd, Cnr Rosedale and Airborne Roads,
Albany, Auckland 1310, New Zealand
Penguin Books (South Africa) (Pty) Ltd, 24 Sturdee Avenue, Rosebank,
Johannesburg 2196, South Africa

Penguin Books Ltd, Registered Offices: 80 Strand,
London WC2R 0RL, England

First published by Plume, a member of Penguin Group (USA) Inc. All essays in
this book were previously published on slate.com, with the exception of the
following: "Chew on This" originally appeared in *The Stranger*; "The Rat
That Roared" originally appeared in *The Wall Street Journal*; "Twenty-Twenty
Foresight" and "After the Fall . . ." are original to this book.

First Printing, June 2003
1   3   5   7   9   10   8   6   4   2

Copyright © Christopher Hitchens, 2003
All rights reserved

℗ REGISTERED TRADEMARK—MARCA REGISTRADA

CIP data is available.
ISBN 0-452-28498-8

Printed in the United States of America
Set in Janson Text

CONTENTS

Preface   **v**

Introduction: Twenty-Twenty Foresight   March 18, 2003   **1**
Arguments for war.

Machiavelli in Mesopotamia   November 7, 2002   **17**
The case against the case against "regime change" in Iraq.

"Armchair General"   November 11, 2002   **20**
The ugly idea that non-soldiers have less right to argue for war.

Terrorism   November 18, 2002   **23**
Notes toward a definition.

Anti-Americanism   November 27, 2002   **27**
Varieties right and left, foreign and domestic.

Imperialism   December 10, 2002   **30**
Superpower dominance, malignant and benign.

Multilateralism and Unilateralism   December 18, 2002   **34**
A self-canceling complaint.

"WMD" and "Inspection"   December 26, 2002   **37**
Are Saddam's weapons really so unconventional?

"Evil"   December 31, 2002   **40**
Scoff if you must, but you can't avoid it.

Prevention and Preemption   January 8, 2003   **43**
When is starting a war not aggression?

"Regime Change"   January 14, 2003   **46**
From evasion to invasion.

Exile and the Kingdoms   January 21, 2003   **49**
Iraq's neighbors want Saddam to flee. Should we?

Chew on This   January 22, 2003   **52**
*Saddam's crimes, al-Qaida massacres, Kurdish freedom, oil
worth fighting for . . . and a few other things Seattle's potlucking
peaceniks might want to think about.*

"Cowboy"   January 27, 2003   **57**
Bush challenged by bovines.

"Recruitment"   February 5, 2003   **60**
Will an Iraq war make our al-Qaida problem worse? Not likely.

The Rat That Roared   February 6, 2003   **63**
On France, the French, Chirac, and the difference between them.

Inspecting "Inspections"   February 13, 2003   **66**
The United Nations is still playing Saddam's game.

"Drumbeat"   February 24, 2003   **69**
Bush rushing to war? Nonsense.

Not Talking Turkey   March 4, 2003   **73**
An ally we're better off without.

Pious Nonsense   March 10, 2003   **77**
The unholy "Christian" case against war.

(Un)Intended Consequences   March 17, 2003   **80**
What's the future if we don't act?

Giving Peace a Chance   April 9, 2003   **83**
The war critics were right—not in the way they expected.

Oleaginous   April 18, 2003   **85**
People who prefer Saddam Hussein to Halliburton.

Epilogue: After the Fall . . .   April 16, 2003   **89**

PREFACE

This is an experiment in the uses of journalism, or perhaps in the usefulness of it, and it's offered with the requisite modesty and arrogance. At the cresting of the international argument over "regime change" in Iraq, when it began to seem that the United States government was finally and seriously committed to the policy, I started to write a series of polemics for the online magazine *Slate*. The idea was to test short-term analyses against longer-term ones, while simultaneously subjecting long-term positions or convictions to shorter-term challenges.

I don't intend to make this exercise seem any more impartial or detached now than it was then. I began from the viewpoint of one who took the side of the Iraqi and Kurdish opposition to Saddam Hussein, who hoped for their victory, and who had come to believe that the chiefest and gravest mistake of Western and especially American statecraft had been to reconfirm Saddam Hussein in power in 1991.

I therefore have not changed anything that I wrote or argued before the intervention that ran from March 20 to April 9, 2003, but rather have submitted it to the critical or objective review of any reader. I have since composed this brief preface and an epilogue. These are dated—and no doubt will date—in the same way as the other contributions. By the time this little book is in anybody's hands, there will have been more developments, forbidding as well as encouraging. One cannot hope to write as a historian about the present, but one can hope to contest, as an essayist, the dishonest, ahistorical view that some events or tendencies that followed the intervention would otherwise never have occurred. However, "In dreams begin responsibilities," and those who kept alive the dream of a free Iraq must accept the responsibility of the logical and probable consequences of their demands. One of the privileges of knowing those who so argued was that they never sought to evade the gravity of this. And that has made all the difference. . . . Thus, I respectfully dedicate this slim work to Barham Salih, Kanan Makiya and Ahmad Chalabi, comrades in a just struggle and friends for life, and to my late friend and colleague Michael Kelly, born on St. Patrick's Day 1957, who was killed on the outskirts of Baghdad International (formerly Saddam) Airport on April 3, 2003.

The original notion, of seeing how such an ephemeral form of words would look in retrospect, came in combination from Jacob Weisberg of *Slate*, Jay Mandel of the William Morris Agency and Trena Keating of Plume/Penguin Books, for whom the longer introduction and epilogue were written. My warm thanks are due to them, to Graydon Carter and Aimee Bell of *Vanity Fair*, who encouraged me to revisit Iraq, and to Piers Morgan and Conor Hanna of the *Daily Mirror*, who published several of my day-by-day comments on the struggle. I am especially obliged to Graydon and Piers, both of whom thought that I was talking rash and dangerous nonsense but neither of whom ever tried to cut me off.

Christopher Hitchens
Stanford, California
April 19, 2003

A Long
Short War

INTRODUCTION
Twenty-Twenty Foresight

ARGUMENTS FOR WAR.

March 18, 2003

On a freezing day of brilliant sunshine in February 2003, I flew to Michigan to watch Paul Wolfowitz, the deputy secretary of defense, attend a Sunday-morning meeting in Dearborn. This town is the home of America's largest Arab-American population, which contains within itself tens of thousands of Iraqi exiles. A local club had opened its public auditorium for as many of these immigrants and citizens as possible to come and question the Pentagon. There was something rather moving about the resulting turnout, in which fluent Iraqi professionals and academics mingled with cardboard-suited cabdrivers, store owners and assembly-line workers who needed some help with the translation. The chair of the proceedings was a poised and elegant Baghdadi woman physician named Dr. Maha Hussain, who headed the cancer-research department at the University of Michigan: Some turbanned Sunni and Shia mullahs sat respectfully in the front row under her direction. Several people in the audience were known to me personally and I was known to some others from having defended the regime-change viewpoint on television. More attendees than I might have guessed were Christian—Chaldean or Nestorian Catholics from the varied confessional weave of Iraq—but this didn't prevent Wolfowitz from opening his remarks with an Islamic greeting (*"as-salaam aleikum"*), and neither did it prevent the Christians and atheists who were present from applauding at least his "inclusive" intentions.

It was Dearborn and not nearby Detroit that provided the launching pad for Henry Ford, to whose name several local buildings and landmarks are still consecrated. Mr. Ford's newspaper, the *Dearborn Independent*, once applied his own technique of mass production to a sinister and paranoid forgery, *The Protocols of the Elders of Zion*, which blamed the ills of the world upon Jewry and made its way from the collapsing scenery of czarist Russia to form the core of aggressive Nazi propaganda. The *Dearborn Independent* serialized this ghastly rubbish, which was later made into a cheap edition and promulgated across the United States and beyond. In the town where this began, I admit that I felt a slight quiver at seeing an enthusiastic Arab crowd gather to acclaim an almost laughably typical Jewish academic and think-tank artist. They had only one question for him, or perhaps two questions in one form. Why have you not already destroyed our tyrant? And can you assure us that you will bring democracy in your wake?

Mr. Wolfowitz has no gift as a demagogue, and he was speaking for a Republican administration and not for himself, but he seemed pleased by the emphasis of these queries and demands. He had been warning against Saddam Hussein, perhaps more in the latter's capacity as an external menace than as an internal despot, since 1978. Indeed, he and some of his colleagues had grown used to being attacked for harboring a grudge against Saddam ("even *before* September 11," as some liked to stress), and wore this distinction as a badge of honor. He did his best to make a level, seminar-like presentation but was repeatedly confronted by questioners with unforgettable stories of torture, murder and humiliation. As far as possible he stuck to the Bush script of U.N.-based legalism, concerning weaponry and resolutions and disarmament. But then as far as he could, he hinted that the administration could be made to care just as much about democracy and emancipation. And he promised that American forces would stay in Iraq no longer than was needed.

Some considerable time before the Dearborn moment, I had decided that the demands of this audience were just. Like many others, I had welcomed the uplifting pro-democracy movement of 1989 symbolized by Tiananmen Square and the subsequent collapse of the mediocre post-Stalinism that had been stultifying Eastern Europe. I had been present for some of the latter drama, during the sanguinary overthrow of the Ceausescu dynasty in Romania. It seemed to me, then, that the old illusion of one-party rule, or one-man rule (or the noxious combination of the two) had been as historically condemned as any theory or practice could possibly be. Having waved good-bye to Franco and Salazar and de Gaulle and Papadopoulos, and then good-bye to Honecker and Husak and the rest, and having also settled accounts with Pinochet and Botha, the civilized world was entitled to some rest and recuperation, and perhaps even a "peace dividend" as the Cold War burned out. Democracy could not be imposed, but it could be released and let grow. Not all weapons would be melted down, but they might become redundant. The U.N. Declaration on Human Rights might be something that could be gradually policed, if not enforced. The humane "non-governmental organizations," which had been so brave in Afghanistan and elsewhere, could take more space and offer an alternative to states and armies and militias.

I feel a bit naive about that now, and somewhat betrayed. It took almost no time for Slobodan Milosevic to transform a dull quasi-socialist failed state into a vivid example of a national-socialist and aggressive one. Saddam Hussein, who always did have a national-socialist ideology, decided that this might be the perfect moment to add the wealth of Kuwait to his dominion. Most sordidly of all, perhaps, the pampered son of Kim Il Sung—the most exorbitantly worshipped despot of our day—strove to outdo the already-flabbergasting cult and menace of his father. The last example is perhaps the most evil (to annex a simplistic term) since Kim Dae-jung of South Korea had braved death and imprisonment throughout the 1980s to transform his country into a functioning democracy and to try and heal the breach of Cold War partition. I had flown home with him on his return trip in 1984, and seen him rearrested but indomitable. He had, when finally elected, put his trust in, and gambled his credit upon, a reciprocal gesture from Pyongyang. And all the time, the leering Kim Jong-Il had been starving his people and forcing them to prostrate themselves before a plutonium god.

Speaking of god, a new mutation of the totalitarian idea was simultaneously collecting momentum. In Afghanistan the Taliban regime had taken the application of *shari'a* law to undreamed-of extremes, forbidding music and destroying all traces of pre-Islamic culture while making women into chattels. Under its protection, the fanatics of al-Qaida were readying themselves for a civil war within the Muslim world, and planning to demonstrate their fitness and daring by exporting this war to the West.

A confrontation with such regimes, in which the citizen is the property of the state and in which only cruelty and cunning are official virtues, seemed unpostponable. Nonetheless, it was postponed as long as possible. There was a general phenomenon of underreaction. Saddam Hussein, even after his crazy aggression of 1990, and even after his defeat in Kuwait, was allowed to remain in control of his republic of fear. Slobodan Milosevic burned and looted and slaughtered his way across Bosnia and Kosovo before finally exhausting the patience of the international community. North Korea was exacting bribes in the form of food aid and even nuclear reactors until detected red-handed in the fraud. The collusion between these three nightmare rulers, by the way, was evident all along. Serbia armed Iraq and vice versa and North Korea timed its "crises" to distract attention from Saddam, and it no more mattered to Baghdad that Milosevic hated and murdered Muslims than it mattered to Serbian fascists that bin Laden detested Christianity. All united in believing that September 11 was a punishment for American hubris. (This mentality was echoed, somewhat more furtively, by many cultural leftists and— somewhat less furtively—by most spokesmen of the hard Right in Europe and America, as well as by many reactionary clerics of all denominations.)

Not all leftist three- or four-word slogans have always been absurd. "No War on Iraq" in 2003 may conceal the silly or sinister idea that we have no quarrel with Saddam Hussein, but the 1930s cry— "Fascism Means War"—is worth recalling. It preserves the essential idea that totalitarian regimes are innately and inherently aggressive and unstable, and that if there is to be a fight with them, which there must needs be, then it is ill-advised to let them choose the time or the place of the engagement. The Bush-Blair strategy for Iraq aimed to arrest and even to reverse a long period of drift and even retreat in this respect, and I am writing this to justify the viewpoint of those who came to agree that this was right.

At the evident risk of seeming ridiculous, I want to begin by saying that I have tried for much of my life to write as if I was composing my sentences to be read posthumously. I hope this isn't too melodramatic or self-centered a way of saying that I attempt to write as if I did not care what reviewers said, what peers thought, or what prevailing opinion might be. Of course one can't always be true to the idea, and I am as capable of seeking laughter or applause or a short-term effect as the next person. Still, I am sincere when I say that the idea of the posthumous never quite deserts me. And I am writing this at a moment in early March 2003 when it's become quite plain that many people have placed their moral and political bets on an American fiasco, or even an American defeat, in what is an imminent yet overdue confrontation in Iraq. I decided some time ago that I was, brain and heart, on the side of the "regime change" position. So I am setting this down, without any throat clearing or on-the-side wagering, to see how it holds up a few weeks from now. I really am making the attempt to argue in the future, as well as about the future. (I notice that as late in the game as March third Thomas Friedman of the *New York Times* has finally lost his nerve, reporting his wife's antiwar misgivings and saying that he was still for the overthrow of Saddam Hussein, but not *this* overthrow. I am fighting to keep my nerve.)

Tonight, for example, I am going to respond to the French foreign minister, M. Dominique de Villepin, on English and French-Canadian TV. Very well, monsieur, I intend to say, is it not the case that French policy is "all about oil"? Does not Saddam Hussein owe vast sums of money to French conglomerates for past sweetheart contracts? And is it not true that the last "independent" policy of Jacques Chirac was the testing of French nuclear weapons in the Pacific, regardless of the wishes of neighboring countries? Did not France also build a nuclear reactor for Saddam Hussein, knowing what he wanted it for? Is it not French policy that is "unilateralist"?

In a way, I regret having to argue at this ad hominem level with a supposedly sophisticated European diplomatist. But what choice do I have, when he says that the "grave consequences" stipulated by U.N. Resolution 1442 should indeed be grave—and should consist of further inspections? Any other policy will be vetoed by France, under any circumstances. Does Monsieur de Villepin imagine that I do not know that Rolf Ekeus of Sweden, proposed by Kofi Annan as chief inspector, was already vetoed by the French delegation to the U.N.? Is it because Ekeus had a record as a serious and committed inspector after 1991, while Hans Blix (the preferred French nominee) had throughout the 1990s certified Iraq and North Korea as good international citizens? After a while, one becomes a prisoner of one's knowledge, and impatient with those who pretend to a naivete that barely covers their evident cynicism.

Since this crisis began, I have become used to arguing with people who say that, if menaced, Saddam Hussein will make use of the genocidal weapons that they usually say he does not possess. I have accustomed myself to hearing that the American oil companies, which wanted to lift even the sanctions on Saddam until recently, are now controlling the White House. I have drummed my fingers while waiting for the opposing speaker to say that this is a war for profit that will also cost far more than we can afford, and can't be a war for democracy in Iraq because it would lead to loud disagreement among Iraqis. Some say that this policy is determined by the fact that America is an empire or a superpower, an observation that would be just as true, or just as relevant, if the United States was intervening on Saddam Hussein's side (as it once did). Some slyly imply that if only the Bush administration had signed the Kyoto treaty—which got exactly no votes in the U.S. Senate—it would have a better chance of persuading people that Saddam Hussein was a menace: one of the great non sequiturs of this debate. Some say that because the United States was wrong before, it cannot possibly be right now, or has no right to be right. (The British Empire sent a fleet to Africa and the Caribbean to maintain the slave trade while the very same empire later sent another fleet to enforce abolition. I would not have opposed the second policy because of my objections to the first; rather it seems to me that the second policy was morally necessitated by its predecessor.) Finally, I keep hearing that Saddam has not attacked the United States and therefore should not be attacked, even though—had Iraq openly done such a thing—there would be no need for the administration to have sought the enforcement of violated Security Council resolutions. It could simply have evoked the clause on self-defense in the U.N. Charter, and done so from the first, instead of trying to restore the vertebrae of international law.

Then I am told daily that this regime-change policy is dictated by an Israeli or Zionist or "Likudnik" lobby. The Israeli government has detested Saddam Hussein since at least 1981, when it blew up the Osirak (or "Oh Chirac") nuclear plant. The same year marked the high point of Reagan's decision to arm and finance Iraq against Iran. So that Jewish influence in Washington seems to explain either everything or nothing in this case, somewhat robbing the theory of any explanatory or analytic force. The fact that many of the neoconservative regime changers have Jewish names is a slightly different observation and somewhat more . . . how shall I put this . . . loaded. Some people take a ridiculously long time to pronounce the word "Jew" and others linger for what seems to me an unnecessarily long time to utter the name Wolfowitz. However, in my twenty-one years in Washington I have noticed that WASPs and Gentiles continue to worm their way, somehow, into the highest positions. And I know that the most strenuous lobbyists for the new Iraq policy have been Iraqis—Arab and Kurdish, Muslim and Christian, secular and devout. The relentless CIA-sponsored attack on Ahmad Chalabi as a sinister banker and financier and conspirator is the closest substitute for the same innuendo and imagery, as applied to a non-Jew, that the other side of this argument has been able to produce.

If the American policy toward Israel is the crucial element here, then it would follow that Saddam Hussein could be guilty of everything that America's critics deny, and yet be immune. Catch Iraq in the very act of importing plutonium or exporting suicide bombers, and the dire fact of the Israeli-Palestine dispute would trump everything. Double standards could still be alleged. Moreover, if nothing can be done about Saddam until the oldest issue before the U.N. has been settled, then an announcement has been made to Baghdad that its regime is safe until Jerusalem is at peace. That's quite a long lease to grant in advance. Meanwhile, of course, Saddam would have every incentive to disrupt such an agreement and thereby prolong his lease. Which he frequently chooses to do. It seems to me wrong to hold Iraqis hostage to the Israeli-Palestinian question, just as it seems to me wrong to hold Israelis and Palestinians hostage to the fluctuations of Saddam's rule.

Striving to rise above this, I am repeatedly pulled down into further crackpot syllogisms that take somewhat longer to refute than they do to utter. But only somewhat. The Bush administration is doing this to distract attention from its failure to crush al-Qaida? How odd, then, that constant official alerts remind the public (in too panicky a way, in my opinion) of the continuing threat. OK then, you can't fight al-Qaida and Saddam at the same time. Really? There's reason to believe that bin Laden may be dead, and many of his cells and lieutenants were rolled up in the fall and spring of 2002/03. In any case, suppose it did turn out to be true, as I believe it is, that Saddam was partly a patron of al-Qaida. Would it have been wise to tell him publicly that we were too busy on one front to do anything about that? (And if Saddam has nothing to do with bin Ladenism, how come his sidekick Mr. Zarqawi, on the run from Afghanistan, managed to take refuge in Baghdad, a city as hard to enter as it is to leave?) One might also observe that Osama bin Laden, or at any rate his voice as ventriloquized by his gang, is overtly pro-Saddam, with a few mad theocratic reservations, and that Saddam couldn't even deny to Dan Rather that he himself basically returned the compliment. As I write, there are still people who mumble ignorantly about Saddam's "secular" regime. Perhaps they have just failed to notice the jihad speeches that he makes every week, the mosques that he builds—often profanely in his own name—and the money he proudly offers to the Islamist suicide-murderers in Palestine.

American foreign policy has long been torn between those "Arabists" who believe that the United States should tilt toward oil-producing powers and those who argue for a strategic alliance with Israel. Now it is asserted that a confrontation with Saddam is driven by both Israel *and* the oil oligarchy. The Israelis might well be relieved to see the end of Saddam, and would have been just as relieved under any government, and never stopped building settlements even during the Camp David/Oslo "peace process." So their position is nothing new, and does not seem to determine that of the United States. Whereas the Saudi Arabians, chief patrons of al-Qaida, are openly hostile to the removal of their buffer-cum-ally in Iraq, and prevented Bush Senior from overthrowing him in 1991. They don't even want their soil used for the intervention. This seems a weird way for the oleaginous faction to express its preference. But one great consequence of a successful regime change in Iraq will be the undermining of the Saudi near-monopoly, as Iraq recovers control over its own natural resources. (By the way, who seriously believes oil isn't worth fighting about?) If this is to be "blood for oil"—and you notice how people employ the term "oil" as if it were some unmentionable bodily secretion, or a foul narcotic that they would never dream of using themselves—then it was even more "blood for oil" when the great powers were doing lucrative deals with Saddam, while he massacred the Kurds and enslaved and tortured the Iraqis.

Since I am writing this in order to be read after what may be a defeat or a disaster, should I spend any time on the "more time" argument? Why not? I am stranded in time, after all. For twelve years, Saddam Hussein has been publicly defecating on the very terms of the U.N.-supervised truce that saved him and his regime. For twelve years, a "no-fly" zone has protected the Kurdish and Shia populations from extermination, and the Anglo-American aircraft enforcing this policy have been under Iraqi ground fire. In other words, the decision to be "at war" with Saddam Hussein was taken a long while ago. Last time, he selected the time and place of the confrontation. Many seem to have argued that he should be allowed the same advantage once more. And since we know that the inspection teams were penetrated by Saddam's secret police, who evidently knew when and where "inspectors" were calling, a demand for more time was really a request for further humiliation, and further proof of impotence.

My jaw has many times dropped on hearing that Saddam Hussein is a "bad guy" all right, but only one among many. Are we or were we to take care of all bad guys, from Robert Mugabe to the Burmese generals? Did the people who said this have *any idea* what they were saying? How many bad guys could they name who had violated the Genocide Convention on their own territory, invaded two neighboring states, openly financed suicide bombing, sought and nearly acquired nuclear capacity and were within easy reach of 9 percent of the world's energy reserves? People say that Saddam understands deterrence and self-preservation—this of a man who blew up the Kuwaiti oilfields *after* he had surrendered them, and after he had been threatened with dire consequences if he did so. A man who not only murders his mildest critics but has also murdered members of his own family and members of his own government. (His foreign minister, Naji Sabry, has seen one brother tortured to death and another merely tortured. His suave deputy Tariq Aziz has seen his son imprisoned for twenty years as a reminder of who is boss. Saddam uses zombies and broken men as his envoys.) The only possible rival here is Kim Jong-Il of North Korea, who can't threaten sea-lanes or commerce very much but who does possess some awesome weapons (the only things in his beggared and enslaved country that may actually work). The same smart-ass critics used to say that double standards were being employed for Saddam and Kim. Yes indeed. But this facile point obscured the fact that Kim actually *has* the deterrent power that Saddam lacks. "More time" was a plea to give Saddam the chance to join the North Korean madman-plus-WMD club, in which case a military intervention in Iraq would have been almost impossible to mount to begin with. Two things I know can happen if inspections give Saddam more time. We know that within a few weeks the North Korean reactors, cynically prepared during a long period of democratization in South Korea, will be ready to assemble and produce plutonium weapons that can be bought off the shelf. We know that a ship carrying concealed North Korean Scud missiles was intercepted in December 2002 as it neared the Yemeni port of Aden. We also know that Yemen needs no Scuds. What might the next secret cargo from Pyongyang to the Gulf be carrying? The second observation is relatively trivial but metaphorically significant. In May 2003, the chair of the U.N. Committee on Disarmament is due to be taken by—Iraq. Perhaps this is what some people are holding out for? I myself continue to hope that by May there will be a government in Baghdad that takes disarmament seriously, and that does not waste its hard-won national income on a parasitic military oligarchy.

That might help in deciding people on the "bad guy" question. In addition to this, I should like to say that the demonstrations I attended or witnessed in London, Washington, San Francisco and elsewhere were actually organized by people who do *not* think that Saddam Hussein is a bad guy at all. They were in fact organized by groups who either openly like Saddam, and Milosevic, and Mugabe, and Kim Jong-Il, or by those who think that Osama bin Laden represents a Muslim cry for help. The fans of the One Party meet the adorers of the One God. Nice work. I kept being told, however, that it was a cheap shot to mention this, because so many perfectly nice people (nuns, teachers, senior citizens) attended the marches in complete innocence. Maybe. But there were just as many housewives, husbands, clergymen, black and Hispanic citizens and ordinary Americans of all stripes among the much more impressive demonstration, consisting of hundreds of thousands of volunteers (you might say civilians in uniform rather than "innocent civilians") who went all the way to the Gulf. To hear from this nice-looking, good-humored and well-mannered rainbow coalition was much more reassuring and confirming than following some blithering ex–flower child or ranting neo-Stalinist through the streets.

Now for another glaring contradiction. If the Bush administration actually went around deposing all bad guys, as the peaceniks taunt it for *not* doing, then that really would constitute preemption. But how preemptive is an intervention in Iraq, when undertaken to enforce a multiply reaffirmed resolution of international law? Saddam has been warned and put on notice and the entire debate on armed enforcement has been exhaustively conducted in full public view. There is no surprise attack being readied here—at least not from the American end. It is true that many of the Pentagon's intellectuals hope for a domino effect from the collapse of Saddam Hussein, extending through Iran and Syria and Saudi Arabia and perhaps Egypt. The worst thing I can say about this is that I devoutly hope it's true. On visits to the region, I have noticed that there is a close if not quite symmetrical fit between the democratically minded and the pro-American. The match becomes closer if one adds the prefix "secular." This is new, not to say shamefully overdue. And before our eyes we have the example of the northern sixth of Iraq, redeemed for over a decade from Saddam's depraved rule. Here we find the beginnings of a multi-party system, with elections, twenty-one newspapers, four female judges, and oil revenues spent on civil reconstruction and not the upkeep of a sadistic junta. This is not Utopia, but neither is it Utopian to say that in Kurdistan (tribal, mountainous, gassed-and-cleansed Kurdistan) regime change has been demonstrated in practice. The real dreamers—or fantasists—are those who think that the status quo in the region can be maintained. That really would risk chaos and disorder. A maimed and traumatized Iraq is in our future no matter what we do: It would be the height of callousness to just let it melt down and see what happened.

In some ways, it has always been something of an exaggeration to describe the impending clash with Saddam as a "war." As the Anglo-American presence in the region grew, it improved the odds that he could be removed without a fight—a contingency that would be unthinkable on the terms proposed by France or Russia. It turned out that this—his resignation or exile—was what many Arab states had wanted all along. In addition, and as an oblique compliment to the many criticisms made by antiwar forces down the years, the Defense Department has evolved highly selective and accurate munitions that can sharply reduce the need to take or receive casualties. The predictions of widespread mayhem turned out to be false last time—when the weapons were nothing like so accurate. Meeting some of the "just war" conditions that used only to be stipulated by Augustine and Aquinas and Grotius, it can now be proposed as a practical matter that one is able to fight against a regime and not a people or a nation.

Incidentally—actually not so incidentally—I hope that the code name for the coming operation does not include the word "Desert" in its title. There is already too much presumption that Iraq is a country of dunes and camels, rather than the highly evolved society that has survived Saddam and will outlive him. I would ban this expression from the discourse along with the claim that when he poisoned and burned Kurdistan Saddam was attacking "his own" people. "His own," as I promised to say for my Kurdish friends, they never have been.

I have saved the most contemptible argument of my opponents until last. If we remove Saddam Hussein, they whimper, we will incur the wrath of those who hate us. Where to begin with this? Perhaps by a thought experiment. If all the claims made by Saddam's enemies were demonstrated as irrefutably true (which as it happens most of them can be) there could and might still be mob rage against any Western intervention in Iraq. It would originate with those who want to restore the lost Islamic caliphate of bin Laden's diseased imagination, and it would be supported by those who think that America is a Jew-controlled casino, as well as by some of the ignorant and the downtrodden. Is there anybody who thinks that we are not *already* at war with the first two factions? How lucky we are that they are so deluded as to identify with Saddam's morbid dictatorship. That's one down to them, not one up. They want to scramble aboard a foundering ship with a crazy captain. I wouldn't save most of them even if I could. Meanwhile, self-respect prevents me from saying that I would shun a policy that risked the anger of al-Qaida. Rather to the contrary, if anything. This is not a confrontation that can be put off. An anthrax bomb in Miami with a clear Iraqi fingerprint would still be explained by the fanatics as a Jewish plot to undermine the devout. Fight them now or fight them later? These two choices are the only ones. Cowering at their potential displeasure is not an option at all, I find I'm glad to say.

In the preceding cases of Serbia and Afghanistan, we were also told that intervention would lead to quagmires, to widespread unrest on the part of the Orthodox in the first case and the Islamic in the second, and all the rest of it. When these alarmist forecasts turned out to be false, the criticism reversed itself. There were still warlords in Afghanistan, became the cry, and bin Laden had not been caught. Such perfectionism, to make any sense at all, would have to demand *more* intervention and not less. Years after the event, those who ordered and carried out the massacre at Srebrenica are still unapprehended, even though they are hiding on European soil. (It seems that more than once, Radovan Karadzic and General Ratko Mladic were tipped off by the French that their arrest was imminent.) However, despite atrocities such as the recent murder of Serbia's prime minister, the condition of every republic in the Balkans is better than it was before the intervention and very much better than it was going to be had Milosevic been able to complete his ethnocidal rampage. I deeply distrust the critics who consistently strive to make the best the enemy of the better, especially when they speak so euphemistically of the worst.

It seems that one needs to say something under the heading of "terrorism," or the support of Saddam Hussein for international gangsterism and nihilism. Imagine if you can the meeting between Saddam and his chief of security on September 12, 2001. The Leader wants to know what is known about those who have just immolated downtown New York, and his secret police chief says, in effect, I've never heard of them O Great One. Never met them either. If that had been his answer, the wretched man would not have lived out the day. Why, of all the groups consecrated to murder and destruction, should Iraq's dictatorship have made an exception in this one case? It would be atypical to say the least. Abu Abbas, whose heroes rolled Leon Klinghoffer's wheelchair off the side of a ship, flew straight to Baghdad and received safe haven. Abu Nidal, who blew up the Rome and Vienna airports and carried out countless other "hits," was an arm of the Iraqi state, not an asylum seeker. Fleeing bin Ladenists found refuge in Iraq *after*, not before, their atrocities in Afghanistan and New York and Pennsylvania and Washington. A related branch of this jihad tendency, removing itself in a hurry from Afghanistan to Kurdistan and naming itself Ansar al-Islam, decided that the main immediate object of religious war should be the assassination of Saddam Hussein's Kurdish opponents. I must be excused if I have a suspicious mind where this coincidence is concerned. But many NATO leaders prefer to analyze it as if the sheer presumption of innocence obtained throughout.

Since one set of my ancestors comes from the west of England and another set from what is now Poland but was once Germany, I have as good a claim to be European as, say, Jacques Chirac has. The governments of Albania (Europe's only Muslim-majority country) and Bulgaria and the Czech Republic—I am only exhausting the ABC—outvote the French and Germans, as it happens, with their support for regime change. But this, though welcome, is beside the point. If Moscow had supported the U.S. position, we would have been taunted for accepting the endorsement of those who put Muslim Chechnya to the sword (and the criticism would have had some validity). The same would be true if Turkey came aboard, which thankfully it seems not to be doing. A principled policy cannot be measured by the number of people who endorse it, whether in transient polls of opinion or by the sterner test of national self-interest, and it has been amazing to me to be told that I must be wrong since I appear to be in a minority. . . .

Try this the other way about: If it was Europe that wanted action and America that did not, as was initially the case in Bosnia and Kosovo, who would get the mandate to take action rather than moan about it? It would be the United States that was called upon to send troops, every time. The spectacle of nations who want influence without any corresponding responsibility is not edifying. If it had been up to them, there would have been no pressure on Saddam to begin with and no means of making good on lawfully shouldered commitments. Don't try and make me too proud of being British (you know how easily embarrassed we are). But I am prouder of my old Labour Party allegiances than I have been for some time. I shall say it shortly: I was pushed out of the Labour Party because of the disgusting support of the Wilson government for Lyndon Johnson's atrocious war on Vietnam. Nothing can make up for that, but Tony Blair's speeches on Iraq ought to embarrass those people—themselves not conspicuously articulate—who snigger endlessly at President Bush's awkward way with words and who imply, in some awful mix of showbiz values with ignorance, that they would have been more persuaded if only the presentation skills of the White House had been smoother.

How absurd, incidentally, that anyone should accuse Blair of being a serf or a ditto or a poodle. He helped propel a reluctant Clinton into the rescue of Kosovo, helped make the original case against Saddam while many Republicans waffled, and in the case of Sierra Leone acted on his own to uphold a treaty that guaranteed that country against a gangster movement of hand-loppers and pirates supported by Liberia and trading (in raw diamonds) with the bankers of al-Qaida. At no point, during the Labour Party conferences or during his addresses to Parliament, did he resort to mere demagogy about supporting British troops simply because they were in harm's way. He always proposed the policy as a matter of principle.

Easy for me to say, you may mutter. I am not going into the desert carrying a pack and a rifle. Certainly not. Nor would any serious army require my enlistment. But I have been in Iraq in time of war, and intend to go again, and if anything has been demonstrated since September 11, 2001, it is that civilians at home are no safer than soldiers abroad in this combat. This brings me to my closing point. On my last visit to Kurdistan I made some friends for life, and I have kept up with them. They, and their allies in the Iraqi democratic opposition, could each tell you a story that would harrow up your soul. You'll get an idea, when the mass graves and secret prisons are opened. Four million Iraqis (out of perhaps twenty-three million) have been forced to take their talents overseas and live in exile. They should have the right of return. For twelve years of compromise and dither, those inside Iraq have been kept by a cowardly international statecraft as hostages in a country used by a madman as his own laboratory and torture chamber. In the face of a modern Caligula, many of them continually risked everything to try and free their people from a system of atrocity and aggression. I feel that they were fighting all this time on my behalf. Only after a long train of blunders and hesitations and betrayals did the United States decide that it was, at long last, in the same trench as the resistance. No matter how it comes out, or how this alliance may fray, I shall never have the least serious doubt that it was the right side to have been on.

Machiavelli in Mesopotamia

THE CASE AGAINST THE CASE AGAINST "REGIME CHANGE" IN IRAQ.

November 7, 2002

Part of the charm of the regime-change argument (from the point of view of its supporters) is that it depends on premises and objectives that cannot, at least by the administration, be publicly avowed. Since Paul Wolfowitz is from the intellectual school of Leo Strauss—and appears in fictional guise as such in Saul Bellow's novel *Ravelstein*—one may even suppose that he enjoys this arcane and occluded aspect of the debate. For those lacking a similar gift for hidden meanings, the best way to appreciate the unstated case for war may be to examine the criticisms leveled by its opponents. These criticisms, which rely on supposed inconsistencies and hypocrisies on the pro-war side, are themselves riddled with contradictions.

First, the opponents of war say, why choose Saddam Hussein when there are so many other bad guys? Second (and related), why exempt Saudi Arabia, which has proven ties to al-Qaida? Third, what about Palestine, for which we already bear a responsibility? Fourth, haven't the Republican establishment, from Dick Cheney to Donald Rumsfeld, been the smiling patrons and financiers of Saddam in the past? There are other points, but you know the tune by now.

Accidentally, this liberal critique helps expose the fact that the chief opponents of a "regime change" strategy are in fact conservatives. They consist of the friends of Saudi Arabia and Turkey (states which likewise oppose the strategy) and of the periphery, at least, of the notorious firm of Kissinger Associates. And they include, as far as we can tell, the president's father. The jeer about Dubya finishing what Daddy began has, you will notice, subsided lately, as Bush Senior's old foreign-policy hands have been signing on with the peacemakers.

Taking the points in order, it's fairly easy to demonstrate that Saddam Hussein is a bad guy's bad guy. He's not just bad in himself but the cause of badness in others. While he survives not only are the Iraqi and Kurdish peoples compelled to live in misery and fear (the sheerly moral case for regime change is unimpeachable on its own), but their neighbors are compelled to live in fear as well.

However—and here is the clinching and obvious point—Saddam Hussein *is not going to survive*. His regime is on the verge of implosion. It has long passed the point of diminishing returns. Like the Ceausescu edifice in Romania, it is a pyramid balanced on its apex (its power base a minority of the Sunni minority), and when it falls, all the consequences of a post-Saddam Iraq will be with us anyway. To suggest that these consequences—Sunni-Shia rivalry, conflict over the boundaries of Kurdistan, possible meddling from Turkey or Iran, vertiginous fluctuations in oil prices and production, social chaos—are attributable only to intervention is to be completely blind to the impending reality. The choices are two and only two—to experience these consequences with an American or international presence or to watch them unfold as if they were none of our business. (I respect those who say that the United States should simply withdraw from the Middle East, but I don't respect them for anything but their honesty.)

Once this self-evident point has been appreciated, it becomes a matter of making a virtue of necessity. If an intervention helps rescue Iraq from mere anarchy and revenge, some of the potential virtues are measurable in advance. The recuperation of the Iraqi oil industry represents the end of the Saudi monopoly, and we know that there are many Wolfowitzians who yearn for this but cannot prudently say so in public. The mullahs in Iran hate America more than they hate Saddam, while Iranian public opinion—notice how seldom "the Iranian street" is mentioned by peaceniks—takes a much more pro-American view. It's hard to picture the disappearance of the Saddam regime as anything but an encouragement to civil and democratic forces in Tehran, as well as in Bahrain, Qatar, and other Gulf states that are experimenting with democracy and women's rights. Turkey will be wary about any increase in Kurdish autonomy (another good cause, by the way), but even the Islamists in Turkey are determined to have a closer association with the European Union, and the EU has made it clear that Turkey's own Kurds must be granted more recognition before this can occur. One might hope that no American liberal would want to demand any less.

In Palestine and Jordan the situation is far more fraught, because loathing for the vile Ariel Sharon has often translated into sympathy for Saddam, and because Saddam has been cultivating the Palestinian rejectionists. However, with his demise this support will have literally nowhere to go, and Chairman Yasser Arafat's discredited entourage will have no serious "rejectionist" option left to them, either. This will be the ultimate test of statecraft: Will a realistic Palestinian acceptance of a territorial solution be reciprocally acknowledged in the form of a dismantling of settlements? By "statecraft" I mean the word literally, since Bush is the first president to have employed the word "state" and "Palestinian" in the same sentence. It is not easy to be optimistic here, but then again there is little to lose, since the so-called Oslo process is a proven failure from the viewpoint either of principle or practice.

From conversations I have had on this subject in Washington, I would say that the most fascinating and suggestive conclusion is this: After September 11, 2001, several conservative policy makers decided in effect that there *were* "root causes" behind the murder-attacks. These root causes lay in the political slum that the United States has been running in the region, and in the rotten nexus of client states from Riyadh to Islamabad. Such causes cannot be publicly admitted, nor can they be addressed all at once. But a slum-clearance program is beginning to form in the political mind.

Iraq is, for fairly obvious reasons, the keystone state here, and it is already at critical mass. Thus it seems to me idle to argue that a proactive policy is necessarily doomed to make more enemies. I have always disliked this argument viscerally, since it suggests that I should meekly avoid the further disapproval of those who hate me quite enough to begin with. Given some intelligence and foresight, however, I believe that an armed assistance to the imminent Iraqi and Kurdish revolutions can not only make some durable friends, it can also give the theocrats and their despotic patrons something to really hate us for.

"Armchair General"

THE UGLY IDEA THAT NON-SOLDIERS HAVE LESS RIGHT TO ARGUE FOR WAR.

November 11, 2002

Continuing with the hidden vernaculars of "regime change," one must pause simply to expel one term, to retire it, discredit it, and make its further employment an embarrassment to those who use it. The word is "armchair."

You've heard it all right. The concept embodied in the contemptuous usage is this: Someone who wants intervention in, say, Iraq ought to be prepared to go and fight there. An occasional corollary is that those who have actually seen war are not so keen to urge it.

The first thing to notice about this propaganda is how archaic it is. The whole point of the present phase of conflict is that we are faced with tactics that are directed *primarily at civilians.* Thus, while I was traveling last year in Pakistan, on the Afghan border and in Kashmir, and this year in the Gulf, my wife was fighting her way across D.C., with the Pentagon in flames, to try and collect our daughter from a suddenly closed school, was attempting to deal with the possibility of anthrax in our mailbox, was reading up on the pros and cons of smallpox vaccinations, and was coping with the consequences of a Muslim copycat loony who'd tried his hand as a suburban sniper. Should things ever become any hotter, it would be far safer to be in uniform in Doha, Qatar, or Kandahar, Afghanistan, than to be in an open homeland city. It is amazing that this essential element of the crisis should have taken so long to sink into certain skulls.

My wife is not of military age, and there is little chance of a draft for mothers. Are her views on Iraq therefore disqualified from utterance? And what about older comrades who can no longer shoulder a gun? What about friends of mine who are physically disabled? Should their expertise—often considerable—be set aside because they can't ram it home with a bayonet?

There are some further unexamined implications of this stupid tactic. It is said, for example, that someone like former Nebraska Senator Bob Kerrey has more right to pronounce on a war than someone who avoided service in Vietnam. Well, last year Kerrey was compelled to admit that he had led a calamitous expedition into a Vietnamese village and had been responsible for the slaughter of several children and elderly people. (He chose to be somewhat shady about whether this responsibility was direct or indirect.) Do I turn to such a man for advice on how to deal with Saddam Hussein?

One hopes that the next implication is inadvertent, but the clear suggestion is that there ought not to be civilian control of the military. What—have callow noncombatants giving brisk orders to grizzled soldiers? How could Lincoln have fired the slavery-loving General George B. McClellan, or Truman dismissed the glorious Douglas MacArthur? During the defense of Washington, Lincoln became the first and last president to hear shots fired in anger. (President Madison was prudent enough to leave before the British burned his house in 1812.) Donald Rumsfeld was at his desk in the Pentagon when the plane hit, but probably is no better and no worse a defense secretary for that.

A related term is "chicken-hawk." It is freely used to defame intellectual militants who favor an interventionist strategy. Senator Chuck Hagel of Nebraska made use of the implication when he invited Richard Perle to be first into Baghdad. Someone ought to point out that the term "chicken-hawk" originated as a particularly nasty term for a pederast or child molester: It has evidently not quite lost its association with sissyhood. It's a smear, in other words, and it is a silly smear for the reasons given above, to which could be added the following: The United States now has an all-volunteer army, made up of people who receive fairly good pay and many health and educational benefits. They signed up to a bargain when they joined, and the terms of the bargain are obedience to the decisions of a civilian president and Congress. Who would have this any other way? If the entire military brass and rank and file opposed a war with Saddam, they would be as obliged to keep their opinions to themselves as they would if they favored nuking Basra. Colin Powell hugely exceeded his authority as chairman of the Joint Chiefs when he wrote articles against the military rescue of Bosnia; he would have been just as open to criticism if he had called for invading Serbia. This is a wall of separation that must not be breached, for the sake of the Constitution. (Mind you, I have the impression that if the "armchair" arguers got their way and asked only war veterans what to do about Saddam Hussein, there would have been a rather abrupt regime change in Iraq long before now.)

When a man thinks that any stick will do, said Chesterton, he is likely to pick up a boomerang. Shall we inquire into the "armchair" or otherwise sedentary lives of those who sympathized with Milosevic, or who published euphemisms about al-Qaida, or who went on fatuous hospitality trips to Baghdad and ended up echoing Baathist propaganda? You can be sure that they would yell about "the politics of personal destruction" or perhaps "McCarthyism" if such an imputation was made. Well, then, let them beware of licensing such a cheap form of ad hominem argument. Just as some of the greatest antiwar writers and poets were courageous soldiers, so some of the best minds of World War II were civilian strategists and code breakers, and some of the finest Resistance fighters were intellectuals who picked up weapons. There is no certain way of enforcing these distinctions morally, until the test actually comes. But now civilians are in the front line as never before, and we shall be needing a more rigorous terminology to reflect that dramatic fact.

Terrorism

NOTES TOWARD A DEFINITION.

November 18, 2002

If any of the terms in our new lexicon has undergone a process of diminishing returns, it is the word "terrorism." This is partly because it is carried over from an earlier lexicon. It is also partly because even that previous lexicon was experiencing a little fatigue, in consequence of the word's ambiguity and hypocrisy. The president himself, declaring us at war with this word, appeared unconsciously to try and hurry us past it, by slurring and condensing it into "terrism" or (it seems on some days) "tourism."

But we need a more exhaustive and exclusive and discriminating definition of it, or recognition of it. The clue may lie in turning the lexicographical pages even further back. In the 1970s, Claude Chabrol produced a brilliant film called *Nada*. It precisely captured both the pointless nastiness and the sinister grandiosity of some of the movements of violence that disfigured that decade. The Baader-Meinhof gang in Germany, the Red Brigades in Italy, the Red Army Faction in Japan—all gave themselves permission to kill, but without any announced goal or objective beyond more of the same. There were other groups in the same epoch, such as the Basque ETA or the Palestinian "Black September," which used unscrupulous and hateful tactics but whose aims could be understood. Chabrol's title, however, recalled an earlier usage for promiscuous cruelty—nihilism. Nothingism. Terrorism, then, is the tactic of demanding the impossible, and demanding it at gunpoint.

I may as well get the obvious out of the way. In London and Belfast during the same period of the 1970s, I was more than once within blast or shot range of the IRA and came to understand that the word "indiscriminate" meant that I was as likely to be killed as any other bystander. I also remember seeing a car bomb explode outside the High Court in London, and I shan't forget a friend of mine being taken hostage by Provisional IRA gangsters. However, at no point in this period did I fail to remind myself that the then British policy in Ireland was stupid and doomed and—much more important—open to change.

The same held, in different degrees, for Zimbabwe and for the Palestinians. It's glib and evasive to say that "one man's terrorist is another man's freedom fighter," because the "freedom fighters" are usually quite willing to kill their "own" civilians as well. But then, so are states. In an excellent essay in *Newsweek*, the conservative Fareed Zakaria points out that as between Russia and the Chechens, there is simply no comparison in the scope and scale and intensity of civilian casualty infliction. Yeltsin and Putin win the filthy prize every time. I hate and despise Hezbollah and Palestinian suicide-murderers, as they ought to be called, but they'd have to work day and night for years to equal the total of civilians killed in Lebanon alone, or by Sharon alone. Lebanese and Palestinian irregulars are, by the way, entitled by international law to resist foreign occupation that has been internationally condemned. Fact. So when Sharon says—as he did on his visit to Ground Zero—that "there is no good terrorism and bad terrorism," he suggests a tautology that operates at his own expense. All parties to all wars will at some time employ terrorizing *methods*. But then everybody except a pacifist would be a potential supporter of terrorism. And if everything is terror, then nothing is—which would mean we had lost an important word of condemnation.

This doesn't mean that we are stuck with some dismal moral equivalence. The IRA or the al-Aqsa Brigades can be reminded, as can states and governments, that some actions or courses of action (bombs detonated without warning in civilian areas; kidnapping; rape) are crimes under every known law. And the evidence is that such awareness, along with some of its moral implications, does become available to them. (The same thought can also be instilled by other less pedagogic means.) Then, of course, you should try and imagine Nelson Mandela or Salvador Allende—leaders of peoples who really did have a beef with the "empire"—ordering their supporters to crash civilian planes into civilian buildings. Excuse me if I say no more, though Mandela was in fact on a Defense Department "terrorism" list as late as the early 1980s.

Now put the case of al-Qaida. Its supporters do not live under a foreign occupation, even if you count the apparently useless and now embarrassing American bases in Saudi Arabia. It is partly a corrupt multinational corporation, partly a crime family, partly a surrogate for the Saudi oligarchy and the Pakistani secret police, partly a sectarian religious cult, and partly a fascist organization. One of its taped proclamations, whether uttered by its leader or not, denounces Australia and celebrates the murder of Australians—for the crime of assisting East Timorese independence from "Muslim" Indonesia! But this doesn't begin to make the case against bin Ladenism. What does it demand from non-Muslim societies? It demands that they acknowledge their loathsome blasphemy and realize their own fitness for destruction. What does it demand for Muslim societies? It demands that they adopt seventh-century norms of clerical absolutism. How does it demand this? By a program of indiscriminate attacks on the civilian population of both. (Yes, both: The Afghan population was reduced by as many Hazara Shiites as the Taliban could manage to kill.) This is to demand the impossible, and to demand it by means of the most ruthless and disgusting tactics.

Enfolded in any definition of "terrorism," it seems to me, there should be a clear finding of fundamental irrationality. Al-Qaida meets and exceeds all of these criteria, to a degree that leaves previous nihilist groups way behind. Its means, its ends, and its ideology all consist of the application of fanatical violence and violent fanaticism, and of no other things. It's "terrorist," all right.

What this means in practice is the corollary impossibility of any compromise with it. It's quite feasible to imagine Hezbollah or Hamas leaders at a conference table, and one has seen many previously "intransigent" forces of undemocratic violence, including the Nicaraguan Contras and the Salvadoran death squads and the Irgun, make precisely that transition. Even Saddam Hussein, who is certainly irrational but was not always completely so, could perhaps have decided to save his life and his regime. But some definitions cannot be stretched beyond a certain point, and the death wish of the theocratic totalitarians, for themselves and others, is too impressive to overlook. One has to say sternly: If you wish martyrdom, we are here to help—within reason.

Anti-Americanism

VARIETIES RIGHT AND LEFT, FOREIGN AND DOMESTIC.

November 27, 2002

In most obvious ways, the term "anti-American" is as meaningless or absurd as the accusation "un-American" used to be. It is both too precise and at the same time too vague. In what other country could one imagine, say, a "House Un-Italian Activities Committee" being solemnly convened? The term "anti-Soviet" was also in wide demagogic use during the Cold War and meant neither "anti-Russian" (let alone "un-Russian") nor, strictly speaking, anti-Communist. The "Soviet," in theory, was the assembly and not the party. But this precedent is discouraging as well.

However, as with other simultaneously overcapacious and overspecific analogues ("terrorism," "anti-Semitism") we do seem to need a word for it. There are those in the Islamic world for whom the slogan Death to America is a real and meaningful invocation. There are those in Europe and elsewhere for whom the word "American" occasions a wrinkle in the nostril. And there are those, in America itself, for whom their country can do no right. I at any rate would claim, perhaps uselessly, to know this phenomenon when I see it.

The United States of America is not just a state or a country but a nation—the only such nation, in fact—supposedly founded on a set of principles and ideas. The documents and proclamations *preceded* the nation-state. China would be China under any regime, and so would Iceland or Egypt, but the USA is also a *concept*. (Rather eerily, I suppose, one could say that this was also partly true of East Germany, North Korea, Israel, Pakistan, and Saudi Arabia—all states based on parties, ideologies, or faiths. But not true in the same way because the United States is based on pluralism as regards faith, political allegiance, or ethnicity.)

That in itself probably explains a certain kind of anti-American style—the kind that expresses contempt for mongrelization and cosmopolitanism. This, which is mixed with both snobbery and racism, is quite commonly found on the European right, which always regarded America as a mobbish and vulgar and indiscriminate enterprise. With some adjustments—resentment at materialism and brashness—it also overlaps with some tropes that can be encountered on the European left. Both mixtures commingle again in Muslim anti-Americanism, which often represents the USA as a sort of racial and commercial chaos, manipulated by cunning Jews.

At the extreme case, which is American imperialism, the most doughty foes of military and political bullying always maintained that they fought against the U.S. government and not the Americans as such. This was the invariable propaganda of the Vietnamese Communists and of Ho Chi Minh himself, who modeled the Vietnamese declaration of independence in 1945 on the well-written preamble of Thomas Jefferson. Probably some of the ridicule that is directed at the idea of anti-Americanism descends from the generation that rightly opposed that war and was falsely accused of being unpatriotic for doing so.

But what if, just for a moment, one tried to classify something as anti-American for its own sake? My nomination would go to Pat Robertson, who appeared on television in the immediate aftermath of the September 11 atrocity and declared that the mass murder in New York and Washington and Pennsylvania was a divine punishment for a society that indulged secularism, pornography, and homosexual conduct. Here is a man who quite evidently dislikes his own society and sympathizes, not all that covertly, with those who would use violence and fanaticism to destroy it. He dislikes this society, furthermore, for the very things that it tends to advertise about itself, namely permissiveness and variety. If this is not anti-American then the term is truly meaningless.

I would go a step further and say that racism and theological bigotry are anti-American as nearly as possible by definition, since these things are condemned or outlawed—after a bit of a struggle, admittedly—in the amendments to the Constitution if not in the document itself. But this would meet with strong objection from some radicals, who suggest that the very idea of America is a fiesta of genocide and slavery dating back to the first contact with Columbus and the Pilgrims. Obviously, both these schools cannot be correct simultaneously. But that would put Americans, for all their conquering history and imperial hubris, in a similar category to that once occupied by other cosmopolitans. If they cannot be accused of plutocracy, for example (or even if they can), they may be accused of subversion, immodesty, and the spread of libertinism and vice, as well as junk food, trash movies, and cheap jeans. It's almost enough to make you proud (except for the food and film bit).

The Cold War succeeded, for a mixture of valid and spurious reasons, in fixing the idea of anti-Americanism as a syndrome of the left. Forgotten was the long hatred of the old right for the American idea. But now we can see its resurgence in the applause from all of the old and new fascist parties for the attacks of September 11. The populist rhetoric against globalization, which is often innocuous enough in every sense, still includes the view of the Le Pens and the Haiders that America is undermining the healthy and organic and familiar "nation-state." So it is indeed, in many ways. More is going on, when the American flag is being burned, than a protest against a superpower. Quite often, especially in some European tones of voice, one can detect a petty resentment of America for being in the right.

As to an appropriate term, what shall we say? With any luck, the American idea is itself too capacious—even too "diverse"—to be wounded by any one insult. But when it comes from outsiders we might learn to say "anti-modernist" or, though it takes a while to utter, "anti-cosmopolitan." From insiders we might derive the notion (not so dishonorable) of "native masochist." I propose these tentatively, knowing full well that they will never catch on. But you will still know them when you see them.

Imperialism

SUPERPOWER DOMINANCE, MALIGNANT AND BENIGN.

December 10, 2002

In the lexicon of euphemism, the word "superpower" was always useful because it did little more than recognize the obvious. The United States of America was a potentate in itself and on a global scale. It had only one rival, which was its obvious inferior, at least in point of prosperity and sophistication (as well as a couple of other things). And both were "empires," in point of intervening in some countries whether those other countries liked it or not, and in forcibly arranging the governments of other countries so as to suit themselves. Still, only a few Trotskyists like my then-self were so rash as to describe the Cold War as, among other things, an inter-imperial rivalry.

The United States is not supposed, in its own self-image, to be an empire. (Nor is it supposed, in its own self-image, to have a class system—but there you go again.) It began life as a rebel colony and was in fact the first colony to depose British rule. When founders like Alexander Hamilton spoke of a coming American "empire," they arguably employed the word in a classical and metaphorical sense, speaking of the future dominion over the rest of the continent. By that standard, Lewis and Clark were the originators of American "imperialism." Anti-imperialists of the colonial era would not count as such today. That old radical Thomas Paine was forever at Jefferson's elbow, urging that the United States become a superpower for democracy. He hoped that America would destroy the old European empires. Jefferson sent a navy to North Africa to confront the piratical Muslim despots who threatened shipping and who seized hostages (and who made cynical separate deals with European powers). Thus "the shores of Tripoli," as celebrated in the opening line of the U.S. Marine Hymn.

This perhaps shows that one should beware of what one wishes for because, starting in 1898, the United States *did* destroy or subvert all of the European empires. It took over Cuba and the Philippines from Spain (we still hold Puerto Rico as a "colony" in consequence) and after 1918 decided that if Europe was going to be quarrelsome and destabilizing, a large American navy ought to be built on the model of the British one. Franklin Roosevelt spent the years 1939 to 1945 steadily extracting British bases and colonies from Winston Churchill, from the Caribbean to West Africa, in exchange for wartime assistance. Within a few years of the end of World War II, the United States was the regnant or decisive power in what had been the Belgian Congo, the British Suez Canal Zone, and—most ominously of all—French Indochina. Dutch Indonesia and Portuguese Angola joined the list in due course. Meanwhile, under the ostensibly anti-imperial Monroe Doctrine, Washington considered the isthmus of Central America and everything due south of it to be its special province in any case.

In the course of all this—and the course of it involved some episodes of unforgettable arrogance and cruelty—some American officers and diplomats did achieve an almost proconsular status, which is why *Apocalypse Now* is based on Joseph Conrad's *Heart of Darkness*. But in general, what was created was a system of proxy rule, by way of client states and dependent regimes. And few dared call it imperialism. Indeed, the most militant defenders of the policy greatly resented the term, which seemed to echo leftist propaganda.

But nowadays, if you consult the writings of the conservative and neoconservative *penseurs*, you will see that they are beginning to relish that very word. "Empire—Sure! Why not?" A good deal of this obviously comes from the sense of moral exaltation that followed September 11. There's nothing like the feeling of being in the right and of proclaiming firmness of purpose. And a revulsion from atrocity and nihilism seems to provide all the moral backup that is required. It was precisely this set of emotions that Rudyard Kipling set out not to celebrate, as some people imagine, but to oppose. He thought it was hubris, and he thought it would end in tears. Of course there is always some massacre somewhere or some hostage in vile captivity with which to arouse opinion. And of course it's often true that the language of blunt force is the only intelligible one. But self-righteousness in history usually supplies its own punishment, and a nation forgets this at its own peril.

Unlike the Romans or the British, Americans are simultaneously the supposed guarantors of a system of international law and doctrine. It was on American initiative that every member nation of the United Nations was asked to subscribe to the Universal Declaration of Human Rights. Innumerable treaties and instruments, descending and ramifying from this, are still binding legally and morally. Thus, for the moment, the word "unilateralism" is doing idiomatic duty for the word "imperialism," as signifying a hyper-power or ultra-power that wants to be exempted from the rules because—well, because it wrote most of them.

However, the plain fact remains that when the rest of the world wants anything done in a hurry, it applies to American power. If the Europeans or the United Nations had been left with the task, the European provinces of Bosnia-Herzegovina and Kosovo would now be howling wildernesses, Kuwait would be the nineteenth province of a Greater Iraq, and Afghanistan might still be under Taliban rule. In at least the first two of the above cases, it can't even be argued that American imperialism was the problem in the first place. This makes many of the critics of this imposing new order sound like the whimpering, resentful Judean subversives in *The Life of Brian*, squabbling among themselves about "What have the Romans ever done for us?"

I fervently wish that as much energy was being expended on the coming Ethiopian famine or the coming Central Asian drought as on the pestilence of Saddam Hussein. But, if ever we can leave the Saddams and Milosevics and Kim Jong-Ils behind and turn to greater questions, you can bet that the bulk of the airlifting and distribution and innovation and construction will be done by Americans, including the new nexus of human-rights and humanitarian NGOs who play rather the same role in this imperium that the missionaries did in the British one (though to far more creditable effect).

A condition of the new imperialism will be the specific promise that while troops will come, they will not stay too long. An associated promise is that the era of the client state is gone and that the aim is to enable local populations to govern themselves. A new standard is being proposed, and one to which our rulers (and we) can and must be held. In other words, if the United States will dare to declare out loud for empire, it had better be in its capacity as a Thomas Paine arsenal, or at the very least a Jeffersonian one. And we may also need a new word for it.

Multilateralism and Unilateralism

A SELF-CANCELING COMPLAINT.

December 18, 2002

Earlier this month, I had a debate on *The Charlie Rose Show* with, among others, Professor Harold Koh. The subject was regime change in Iraq and the related question of intervention in its favor. (If the name Harold Koh is unfamiliar to you, it is because he was President Clinton's undersecretary for human rights.) In the course of the exchanges between us, he must have pronounced the word "multilateral" or "multilateralism" several dozen times. Whoever taught him these terms did a thorough job. He could fit them into any sentence at any time. If he will allow me to summarize his view (and the transcript would bear me out here), Professor Koh had nothing much against regime change or indeed against intervention, so long as it was brought about in a multilateral manner.

One could have stooped, of course, and been "partisan." The Clinton administration, served by Koh, allowed itself to bomb Sudan without demanding inspections, without resorting to the United Nations, without consulting Congress, and without even telling several of the Joint Chiefs. The same administration bombed Baghdad from the day that the impeachment trial of the president began until the day that the trial was over, again without troubling to pass any of the above tests. In another episode, Madeleine Albright was instructed to veto a Czech motion calling for strengthening U.N. forces in Rwanda in order to "preempt" the genocidal plan prepared by Rwanda's racist government.

But let us rise above such petty temptations. If the United States had supported the Czech proposal, then that proposal would have automatically ceased to be unilateral and become, just like that, bilateral or (since bilateral carries the implication of two contrasting parties) well on its way to becoming multilateral. That's if you agree to forget that multilateral means "many-sided," whereas the recruitment of more nations or forces to any one "side" means that the cause may remain "one-sided" but has at least succeeded in attracting multiparty or multiple-country support.

Tautology lurks here. In October, I went to speak at a meeting at the Labour Party conference in Blackpool, England. Tony Blair had carried the day in the plenary session, but many delegates were muttering darkly about the "unilateral" or "go-it-alone" attitude of the United States. I suggested that, if this was indeed the problem, the solution was ready at hand. Simply support the U.S. position against the Iraqi or Russian or French one and—presto—the U.S. position would no longer be unilateral. I was promptly made aware of what I already knew—that the true objection to the policy has little to do with its unilateral character.

The supporters of German chancellor Gerhard Schröder were the next to make the same mistake. Of course, they said, something must be done about Iraq. But how can America expect to do this without European support? A good question, but posed by people who would not stay for the answer. The most dada version of the dilemma was stated by Senator Tom Daschle, who for weeks appeared to say that if only more people would endorse the president's policy, why then, he might be induced to support it himself! But in the meanwhile, he could only frown upon anything unilateral.

This self-canceling complaint echoes the nondistinction on Capitol Hill between the terms "partisan" and "bipartisan." A proposal is partisan if made by one party, but becomes bipartisan (while remaining exactly the same as a proposal) if it is endorsed by enough members of the other party. There's no trick to it really. It's all a matter of wooing rather than principle.

Thus, the United Nations is committed—multilaterally if not unanimously—to an inspection program backed by the threat of force, which had to originate somewhere and was actually put forward—therefore unilaterally by definition—by the American team. But does that stop anyone from persisting in saying that the implied other shoe of enforcement must not be unilateral either? Apparently it does not. Thus, an accusation of unilateral behavior can be made to stick, almost by axiom, by any power that withholds consent. When that consent is eventually given, the prize of multilateralism has been attained, again by definition. But the charge of acting unilaterally may not, for some reason, be laid against (say) France.

There are diminishing returns to this false antithesis. And they partly arise from the sad fact of its being a false definition in the first place. The American attitude toward the Middle East could well be one-sided and still enjoy or attract wide support from other countries. A majority can in theory and practice act one-sidedly, just as a single state may have more respect for pluralism than a dozen rival states put together.

This also raises the related question of how decisions are actually made. The Syrian vote on the crucial U.N. resolution was not a fragment or component of another country's vote. It was a decision made, at least to all outward purposes, by Syria alone and for reasons congruent with Syrian interests. And this is Syria's perfect right. What could be more unilateral than that? But the vote happened to coincide with the expressed views of fourteen other delegations, which gave it a nice multilateral feel. Yet the Iraqi delegation, for some reason, has been flagrantly in breach of a number of overwhelmingly passed resolutions for more than a decade. And yet one never seems to read any well-reasoned denunciation of this unilateralist attitude on the part of Baghdad. Add another clause to the regime-change manifesto: Intervention will put an end to Saddam Hussein's unilateralism.

Part of my intention in writing this has been to make the reader thoroughly sick of both terms, and sick of the empty usage to which they have been put. Are you sick yet? I predict that you soon will be.

"WMD" and "Inspection"

ARE SADDAM'S WEAPONS REALLY SO UNCONVENTIONAL?

December 26, 2002

In the summer of 1991, I went to the Kurdish city of Halabja for *National Geographic* magazine. This is the town that's now world famous for being hit by Iraqi chemical weapons. The effects of such tactics are mainly instantaneous—hence the celebrated picture of hundreds of families lying in the street as if an angel of death had done a drive-by—but the longer-term fallouts are quite arresting, too. Women, in a region celebrated for modesty, could roll up their heavy skirts to show horrifying burns. People were blind. Children were in semi-autistic states. One unexploded weapon, bearing Iraqi air force markings, was still lodged in the rubble of a basement, and I possess a photograph of myself sitting gingerly on top of it.

Was Halabja, however, struck by a "weapon of mass destruction"? Although the answer may seem self-evident, actually most of the city and many of its inhabitants are still there. A sustained day of carpet bombing with "conventional" weapons would have been more lethal, as well as more annihilating. And an attack with anthrax- or smallpox-tipped devices would still have left the buildings intact, as neutron bombs are also supposed to be able to do.

The term "WMD," then, appears to be both an over- and understatement. It can overstate the destructive power of some weaponry, while understating its wickedness. The two most destructive moments of the last Gulf War were, in point of casualties, the revenge taken by Saddam on the Shia and Kurdish intifada in the conflict's closing moments; in point of physical mayhem, his decision to ignite the Kuwaiti oilfields during Iraq's ignominious retreat. The main weapon in the first instance was the helicopter gunship, and the chief one in the second instance was high explosive. Mass destruction of humans and resources was the outcome in each case, but this tells us little about the weaponry (while telling us a good deal about the regime).

The phrase "weapons of mass destruction" originated, as far as I can tell, as a Soviet expression during the protracted '70s and '80s negotiations about arms control and détente. It was a generalization, as well as something of a euphemism, but it was also a loosely pejorative way of referring to thermonuclear weaponry. That kind of warfare obviously meets all conditions of condemnation, because it causes unimaginable damage to cities and to the infrastructure, as well as vaporizing civilians by the million and tearing apart the web of nature that we call the ecology. Insofar as we can tell, it also threatens the whole biosphere and creates long-term risks from radiation and climatic change. At its worst, it could cause extinction rather than mere extermination: killing everybody alive, as well as those yet unborn—a true and apocalyptic "end of history." No gas or bug or nerve agent can quite do that.

Slightly fatuous though it may be to admit it, we probably draw back from words like "gas" and "chemical" because, like the term "germ warfare," they seem sinister and underhanded. They supply a rhetorical means of hissing at the villain and his ghastly laboratory. The use of gas in the trenches of World War I is part of a folk-memory of horror (and it also presaged the use of vermin-killing methods on civilians, which along with its racism is what makes the concept of the Final Solution so rank and disgusting). However, if we are to try to be objective about it, the use of gas is not more grossly destructive than the use of incendiary and blockbuster bombs to create an urban firestorm, as was done in Tokyo and Dresden. Disease warfare, repellent as it may be, is unstable and tricky and dependent on methods of dissemination that tend to require sophisticated and accurate missiles.

It is very obvious that Saddam Hussein has tried to acquire the only real WMD—the thermonuclear type—and it's fairly apparent (to me at any rate) what he wants them for. The best evidence is that he has failed in this enterprise, while a good intuition would suggest that having sacrificed so much in the quest he is unlikely to give it up. So, one justification for his removal might be the simple statement that he will never find out what it feels like to be a nuclear dictator. That would be a justification somewhat blunter than any the Bush administration has felt able to advance. The official pretense is that methods of supervision will both disclose and preempt the threat. Possible, but improbable.

Responsibility for this pretense is shared by those who trust the idea of "inspection" and those who take the word at its face value. There's a potentially nice coincidence between the notion of inspection and the work of epidemiology: Good hygiene counters the epidemic. But these things require reciprocity. Who on earth submits to the ministrations of a doctor and, in response to his questions, tries to make him guess where the pain is? ("You didn't ask the right question!") The correct treatment for a regime of sadism and megalomania like Saddam's is more akin to the "committal" procedure adopted for those whose mental disturbance is a menace to themselves and others. ("Take your meds and then we'll have a long, long talk.") That's why inspection has had to be enforced upon him in the first place. The existence of weapons of indiscriminate destruction, or weapons of mass terror, might be inferred from the profile of any modern government. The threat they might constitute could only be inferred by a close study of that government itself. And you could not properly inspect or diagnose Iraq, after all that's been endured and discovered, without being in control of it. Thus, those who emphasize WMDs might as well be honest and admit that they are talking partly about latency. And those who sincerely want to see a genuine invigilation ought to confess that inspection is only another demand for (and condition of) regime change.

"Evil"

SCOFF IF YOU MUST, BUT YOU CAN'T AVOID IT.

December 31, 2002

There is probably no easier way to beckon a smirk to the lips of a liberal intellectual than to mention President Bush's invocation of the notion of "evil." Such simplemindedness! What better proof of a "cowboy" presidency than this crass resort to the language of good guys and bad guys, white hats and black hats? Doesn't everybody know that there are shades and nuances and subtleties to be considered, in which moral absolutism is of no help?

Apparently everybody does know that, since at election times the same liberal intellectual will, after much agonizing, usually cast his vote for whichever shabby nominee the Democratic Party throws up. And he will do so, in his own words, because this is "the lesser *evil.*" So, it seems that we cannot quite do without the word, even though it's worth noticing that some people only employ it in an ironic or relativist sense, as a quality that must be negotiated with, accommodated, or assimilated.

Though the word is often heard on the lips of preachers and moralists, it does also figure in the reflections of modern moral philosophers. Faced with the evidence of genocidal politics in twentieth-century Europe, Hannah Arendt, for example, posed the existence of something she termed "radical evil" and suggested that intellectuals were failing to allow for its existence as a self-determining force. Her phrase "the banality of evil" also enjoys wide currency, serving to help us understand the ways in which "ordinary men" can be mobilized or conscripted to do exceptionally ghastly things. If she had said "radical sinning" or "the banality of sin" she might have seemed sermonizing or naive, but then President Bush did not refer to an "axis of sin," did he?

It may not be of much help, in propaganda terms, to describe an enemy as evil. Time spent in understanding and studying a foe is always time well spent, and absolutist categories may easily blunt this rigorous undertaking. But how far can certain analyses be taken without running up against a recurrence of Arendt's dilemma?

Everybody knows that morality is indissoluble from the idea of conscience and that something innate in us will condemn murder and theft without having to have the lesson pedantically inculcated. Finding a full wallet on the backseat of a cab and deciding to hang on to it, most people would have to subject themselves to at least some rationalization and justification, even if they were sure that nobody had detected them. I myself can't decide if this inherent conscience is conferred upon us by evolutionary biology—in other words, whether it selects well for socialization and survival and thus comes to us as something possessing evident utility. That thought might be merely as comforting as a belief in altruism. However, I do know for sure that a certain number of people manage to be born, or perhaps raised, without this constraint. When confronted with the unblinking, conscienceless person we now say that he is a psychopath, incapable of conceiving an interest other than his own and perhaps genuinely indifferent to the well-being of others.

This diagnosis is certainly an advance on the idea of demonic possession or original sin. But not all psychopaths are the same. Some, rather than being simply indifferent to the well-being of others, have an urgent need to make others feel agony and humiliation. Still others will press this need to the point where it endangers their own self-interest—just as a pathological liar is one who utters apparently motiveless falsehoods even when they can do him no possible good. Thus, we have to postulate the existence of human behavior that is simultaneously sadistic and self-destructive. We would not have much difficulty in describing the consequences of such behavior as evil. "It was an evil day when . . ." "The evil outcome of this conduct was . . ." Why, then, is there any problem about ascribing these qualities to the perpetrator?

For example, many countries maintain secret police forces and in-

flict torture on those who disagree. And some countries inflict torture
or murder at random, since the pedagogic effect on the population is
even greater if there is no known way of avoiding the terror. Caprice,
also, lends an element of relish to what might otherwise be the bor-
ing and routine task of repression. However, most governments will
have the grace (or the face) to deny that they do this. And relatively
few states will take photographs or videos of the gang rape and torture of a young woman in a cellar and then deposit this evidence on
the family's doorstep. Such eagerness to go the extra mile, as is manifested in Saddam Hussein's regime, probably requires an extra degree
of condemnation. And if we are willing to say, as we are, that the devil
is in the details, then it may not be an exaggeration to detect a tinc-
ture of evil in the excess. We could have a stab at making a clinical definition and define evil as the surplus value of the psychopathic—an
irrational delight in flouting every customary norm of civilization.

Like everything else, including moral relativism, this would be
subjective. Probably no journalist has had more fun denouncing Bush
as a reactionary simpleton than Robert Fisk of the London *Independent*. His dispatches have an almost Delphic stature among those who
decry American "double standards." Yet I still have my copy of the article he wrote from Kuwait City soon after the expulsion of Saddam's
forces. He described as best he could the contents of certain cellars
and improvised lockups and the randomness of the carnage and destruction and waste (remember that Saddam blew up the Kuwaiti oilfields when he had already surrendered control of them), but there
was an X factor in the scene that he could smell or taste rather than
summarize. "Something *evil*," he wrote, "has happened here." I think
I agree with him that we do indeed need a word for it, and that this
is the best negative superlative that we possess.

Prevention and Preemption

WHEN IS STARTING A WAR NOT AGGRESSION?

January 8, 2003

It is said that during the 1973 Yom Kippur War—known on the other side as the Ramadan War—an Israeli military spokesman was asked for the fourth or fifth time whether the Jewish state would use nuclear weapons if its ground forces continued to suffer defeat. He repeated the official mantra—"Israel will not be the first country to deploy nuclear weapons in this region"—and then stepped back from the microphone (which he believed to have been switched off) and whispered to himself, "And we won't be the second one, either."

Warfare is an enterprise where, very noticeably, nice guys finish last. Franklin Roosevelt famously and pugnaciously said, after the "day that will live in infamy" in 1941, that it would count in the end not who fired the first shot but who fired the last shot. Nonetheless, it hurts to begin a war with the loss of a fleet, and not all countries are big enough to sustain such a shock. As a result, military historians and military strategists spend a good deal of time arguing over "preemptive" war and its near cousin "preventive" war.

Most of this discussion is impossibly abstract and subject to the rule of blind contingency. The only certain way of preventing World War II, for example, would have been for the Germans to have won World War I. (Because this outcome would have forestalled the rise of Nazism.) But the British and French military planners of 1918, with their American allies, could obviously not be induced to see things that way. The other, rather belated, way of preventing World War II from becoming a world war would have been a united front between Britain, Russia, and France to crush the Hitler-Mussolini forces before they could get properly started. It's not as if there would have been a shortage of pretexts. But then many Germans to this day would be insisting that their country had been a victim of aggression, and the political consequences of that might have been nasty as well.

The U.N. Charter reserves to all member states the right to use unilateral force if they can invoke the clause that specifies self-defense. But this means by definition that an aggressor must have shown his hand and initiated a war before any compensating or retaliatory action can be taken. Some nations don't care to be branded as "aggressors" and will go to some trouble to avoid the charge, but in general it's a bit like the old No Spitting signs that I used to see on British buses. Who, likely to expectorate on public transport, will be deterred from doing so by a notice? These injunctions apply only to those who would obey them without being told.

Take the extremely flammable situation along the Indo-Pakistan frontier. Pakistan is much smaller than India and has a much smaller army. It also has a "waist," geographically speaking, which means that a sudden Indian "conventional" strike could punch across the border, cut Pakistan in half, and separate its capital city, Islamabad, from its only seaport in Karachi. It is this strategic nightmare that determined the Pakistanis on the acquisition of a nuclear capacity, with which they could destroy Indian armor and infantry as it was massing. Which side would then be the aggressor? The one that was massing, or the one that vaporized the potential assault force? In the early Clinton years, the Pakistanis became sure that they were about to be attacked and prepared to launch, and the American officials who stopped the clock with only minutes to go are still inclined to shiver as they recall the moment. General Pervez Musharraf has since boasted publicly that if India had taken one extra step over the Kashmir question in late 2001, he would have ordered a preemptive nuclear attack. But this demented logic holds for all nuclear powers, all of whom are aware that the only real use for such devices is in an overwhelming first strike.

Israel's classic preemptive war in June 1967, which destroyed the Arab air forces on the ground, was also justified as preventive because it stopped an attack before it could get started. But the Nasser side could and did reply that in 1956 Israel had attacked without any such provocation, so this was just their slow-motion retaliation for an original first strike. Winston Churchill spent much of his career hoping to entice Germans or Japanese into attacking American ships, the better to lure them into war with the United States and then get the United States to declare for Britain. This was preemption of a high order, by means of proxies who unwittingly did what was wanted of them and widened the war in order to shorten it.

In the present case of Iraq, a preemptive war is justified by its advocates on the grounds of past Iraqi aggressions and the logical presumption of future ones—which would make it partly retaliatory and partly preventive. This is fraught with the danger of casuistry since if no sinister weaponry is found before the war begins, then the war is rejustified on the grounds that it prevented such weapons from being developed. (And if some weapons are found, as one suspects they will be, after the intervention has taken place, then they could be retrospectively justified as needful for defense against an attack that was obviously coming.)

Surveying the bloody past, one can only wish for the opportunity to rerun the tape so that enough judicious force could have been employed, in good enough time, to forestall greater bloodshed. Everyone will have their favorite example. If only, for instance, the U.N. troops in Rwanda had been beefed up and authorized to employ deadly force as a deterrent. But tautology lurks at every corner, and the distinction between preemptive and preventive becomes a distinction without a difference, and only hindsight really works (and not always even then). The lesson is that all potential combatants, at all times, will invariably decide that violence and first use are justified in their own case.

"Regime Change"

FROM EVASION TO INVASION.

January 14, 2003

Of all the terms in the argument about war with Saddam Hussein, perhaps the most protean and slippery is "regime change." This is not all that surprising when you reflect that it has its origins in those heavily parsed years that we can never quite bring ourselves to call the Clinton era. The words became current during the debate over the passage of the Iraq Liberation Act, which was sponsored by Senators Lieberman and Kerrey (the Nebraska one) and which passed without a dissenting vote.

This legislation committed the United States to support the removal of Saddam Hussein by the exercise of any force but its own. The plan was to identify Iraqi and Kurdish groups that merited support and to endow them with money for propaganda and rebellion. In one stroke, it also neatly squared an awkward circle: The administration and Congress could be identified with a hawkish (or perhaps hawk-*ish*) line on Iraq without risking the lives of any Americans or interrupting Clinton's fatuous attempt to earn himself a Nobel Prize for settling the Israel-Palestine dispute.

"Regime change" expressed this ambiguity and some others as well. What could seem more inoffensive than proposing a change of government—and furthermore, leaving it all up to the Iraqis? Isolationists and interventionists could vote for the same measure without having to identify their differences. But this soft option deliberately obscured the salient fact that an alteration of regime in Iraq could only come about by means of *(a)* insurrection; *(b)* invasion; or *(c)* military coup. The Iraq Liberation Act did not involve paying Frank Luntz or Dick Morris to see what the "numbers" would be for the new third party Shiite Centrist Coalition, as it attempted to bridge the gender gap in the swing-state Basra region.

It is now admitted by all concerned that only the force of American arms, or the extremely credible threat of that force, can bring a fresh face to power in the evidently rather jaded Baghdad political scene. The closer political metaphor would be "new blood"—and perhaps quite a bit of it.

Insurrection has been tried, by the Kurdish forces in the north for many decades and also by the Shiite population in the south, which launched an intifada after the last Gulf War. (Opinions differ on how much that rebellion was incited by American broadcasts from Saudi Arabia and on how many direct and indirect promises were made to the rebels by the United States.) Saddam Hussein's relative command of the air and his willingness to use mass-reprisal tactics more or less ensured then, as they ensure now, that he cannot be overthrown by a mere revolt. However—and this has become important—the imposition of the Anglo-American "no-fly" zones to protect the Kurds and Shiites from further massacre has meant that, in a way, we are already in a state of war with Saddam Hussein. (The no-fly zones do not have U.N. authority.)

There is another consideration. Not only did the Shiite rebels exact terrible revenge on local Baath Party officials and others whom they suspected of collaboration, but some of them have ties to the less liberal elements within Iran. Were things permitted to run their course, there could be a regime change of a sectarian, localized kind.

The idea of a coup at the center has always been much more attractive to American officialdom, especially during the Clinton period. And after all, military coups are what the CIA does best. Why, the agency even involved itself in the very coup that helped bring Saddam Hussein to power . . . but this again raises the limitations of the "regime change" idiom. Another friendly general, perhaps without a mustache but most probably a member of the Sunni minority (if not of the Tikriti minority of the Sunni that gave us Saddam himself), might be ideal from Washington's point of view. If he could conveniently hoist or shoot himself into power in the next few weeks, he could even obviate the need for a messy full-scale intervention. This is what many Iraqi dissidents are calling "the nightmare scenario"—a last-minute thwarting of the project for a totally renovated system. Some of them even refer to it as "Saddamism without Saddam," though that increasingly looks like a contradiction in terms.

Thus the logic of regime change has come to mean less and less a secondhand involvement in a proxy struggle waged by other people, and more and more a direct and avowed engagement in the enterprise of invading and then remaking someone else's country. At one point last year, the president seemed to say that full Iraqi compliance on disarmament would in fact constitute "regime change" and would thus allow a declaration of victory. That moment now seems rather distant. Instead, he finds himself meeting in the Oval Office with men and women who proclaim that they want a pluralist, secular, constitutional Iraq. He need only supply the muscle.

Barham Salih, the brave gentleman who is currently the elected prime minister of Iraqi Kurdistan, told me that of the two historic examples of American involvement in "nation-building," he prefers the instance of Germany over Japan. "In Japan too much of the old order was left in place. In Germany there was de-Nazification." This would be more like revolution from above or what colonial idealists used to call "the civilizing mission": everything from the education system to the roads. Nobody should underestimate for a second what the magnitude of the task is. But we still persist in employing a clever euphemism, which was designed precisely to obscure that task, and its magnitude, from our gaze.

Exile and the Kingdoms

IRAQ'S NEIGHBORS WANT SADDAM TO FLEE. SHOULD WE?

January 21, 2003

Previously I wrote of one possible version of regime change—the preservation without Saddam Hussein of the Sunni Muslim (actually Tikriti) military authority in Iraq—as the "nightmare scenario" of the Kurdish forces and the more democratic Iraqi dissidents. A version of this same scenario is now being discussed, and even endorsed by administration nodders and winkers, on the apparently humane grounds that it would obviate the necessity for war.

Actually, abdication without invasion could be justified on more exalted grounds than that. If Saddam Hussein could be induced to surrender his personal dictatorship and leave his martyred country for a presumably secure but this time disclosed location, it would demonstrate that the mere threat of force, if convincing enough, could achieve astonishing results. Quite evidently, the Turkish and Saudi Arabian and Egyptian regimes would not be adopting this latest rather noisy form of quiet diplomacy if they were not persuaded that the alternative was military intervention. Q.E.D., in a way, for the hawks, with a generously deferential nod to the doves and the allies and the United Nations.

However, this happy-seeming outcome would leave two factions with gritted teeth, for different reasons. In the minds of the tougher thinkers at the Defense Department in particular, the whole point of removing Saddam Hussein is to inaugurate a wave of change in neighboring states as well. Thus a victory over Saddamism that skips this critical demonstration is a somewhat hollow one, especially if the "skip" is undertaken at the request of the very regimes—most notably the Saudi—that were the undeclared but definite targets of the demonstration in the first place.

Then there are those who have worked tirelessly and at great risk to change not merely the government of Iraq but the Iraqi system of government. It would be a mistake to view this in theological terms only. After all, the Kurds are just as Sunni as Saddam Hussein, if not indeed more so. More to the point is the complex and ambitious plan, proposed by Kanan Makiya on behalf of the Iraqi opposition at its rather fractious London summit, to declare Iraq a multicultural and multiethnic pluralism, defined neither as Arab or Muslim but as constitutional.

The follow-up meeting to this conference, a gathering of Iraqi exiles and oppositionists to be held in the Kurdish town of Suleimaniyah, was abruptly called off by its Bush administration supporters on the rather odd grounds of security. This can't have been a truly serious objection, since the town has been within muzzle range of Saddam for some time and was thus either too risky to begin with or no more risky than before. The likelihood that Saddam would decide to shell or bomb the town during a meeting between the Bush administration and his local enemies—an action which, if taken, would offer the perfect pretext for an invasion—must be accounted pretty slight, at least before the January inspection deadline kicked in.

If talk of a relatively painless and vestigial change of regime doesn't come from the Defense hawks and doesn't come from the Iraqi opposition in exile, whence does it arise? The suspicion emerges that there is some covert diplomacy at work, designed to accommodate the local and regional oligarchies and the waverers at the United Nations. The concept of Saddam removing to some sort of exile (which in my memory was first "floated" by the foreign minister of Qatar last September) is not despicable on its face. It would avert the possibility of even the smartest bombs going astray and hitting orphanages, and it would mean that Iraqi soldiers would not be ordered pointlessly to their deaths by a deranged Caligula. It would also remove the chance of some final apocalyptic lunge on Caligula's part.

Moreover, the next Iraqi regime would certainly need a lot of help with security, law and order, civil reconstruction, and food and medical aid. So, the forces of the coalition would most probably be "invited" in to provide some of this support and to secure the oilfields from sabotage or worse, as well as to identify and destroy some conspicuous weapons "sites." It would still count as a great deliverance for the Iraqi people. President Bush would be in an especially strong political position, at home and abroad, for achieving a version of "peace through strength" and for avoiding the charge of "cowboy" tactics.

However, it would be nice to have some sense in advance of what the price of this deliverance might be. The argument for unconditional surrender in previous conflicts was, first, that it insisted that further resistance was futile and, second, that it did not necessitate the degrading business of bargaining with war criminals and fascists. Since the best moral argument for regime change in Iraq is based upon the horrific way in which the Iraqi and Kurdish peoples have been treated, one would like to know how much water is being added to the wine here. Is Saddam Hussein to be granted perpetual immunity? Is Ali Hassan al-Majid, the butcher of Kurdistan and Kuwait, to escape the trial that he so conspicuously needs? (He is currently touring Syria, Jordan, and Egypt as an Iraqi roving delegate, and it is to the shame of all those governments that they do not place him immediately under arrest.) Are we expected to look the other way if some capital offers protective hospitality to Saddam, as we now officially pretend that Saudi Arabia is not sheltering Idi Amin? Moreover, what do we say to the numberless Iraqis and Kurds who will wish to seek redress or information about their missing relatives, or compensation for their violated property and lives?

I personally never ask myself what would Jesus do, and if I did I hope I would have the self-possession to say that I had no idea. In any case he was and is a quasi-mythical figure. Saddam Hussein and his gang are corporeal and material in the extreme, and they believe that it takes a regime to protect them from what they have done. If the regime is changed, as it obviously will be soon, one way or another, then life should change abruptly for them, too. The point of the change is to instate some standard, however tenuous and hypocritical, of international law. One can not easily achieve that by exempting its chief violators to begin with. The Kissinger principle—the greater the crime the greater the immunity—would be a shabby reward to those who have borne the heat and burden of the day.

Chew on This

SADDAM'S CRIMES, AL-QAIDA MASSACRES,
KURDISH FREEDOM, OIL WORTH FIGHTING
FOR . . . AND A FEW OTHER THINGS
SEATTLE'S POTLUCKING PEACENIKS
MIGHT WANT TO THINK ABOUT.

January 22, 2003

Dear brothers and sisters, boys and girls, comrades and friends,
The editor of your local alternative rag, *The Stranger*, told me of
your upcoming "Potlucks for Peace" event and invited my comments,
and at first I couldn't think of a thing to say. For one thing, why
should I address a Seattle audience (or even suppose that I have a
Seattle audience, for that matter)? I daresay that I can claim a tenuous connection, because I have always had a good crowd when reading at the splendid bookstores of the city, and because it was in Seattle
that I stayed when grounded on September 11, 2001, a date that now
makes some people yawn.

I had been speaking to the students of Whitman College in Walla
Walla about the crimes of Henry Kissinger and had told them that
September 11—which was then tomorrow—was a symbolic date. On
that day in 1973, the civilian government in Chile had been drowned
in blood by an atrocious military coup. On the same day in 2001, a
group of Chilean survivors proposed to file a lawsuit against Kissinger
in a federal court in Washington, D.C. I showed a film illustrating
this, made some additional remarks, and closed by saying that the
date would be long remembered in the annals of the struggle for
human rights. I got some pretty decent applause—and this from the
alma mater of Henry "Scoop" Jackson, whose family was present. On
the following morning I got a very early call from my wife, who was

three hours ahead of me. She told me to turn on the TV, and she commented mordantly that the anti-Kissinger campaign might have to be on hold for a while. (Oddly enough, and as recent events have shown, she was mistaken about that.) Everyone knows what I saw when I turned on the TV.

Now hear this. Ever since that morning, the United States has been at war with the forces of reaction. May I please entreat you to reread the preceding sentence? Or perhaps you will let me restate it for emphasis. The government and people of these United States are now at war with the forces of reaction.

This outcome was clearly not willed, at least on the American side. And everybody with half an education seems to know how to glibly dilute the statement. Isn't Saudi Arabia reactionary? What about Pakistani nukes? Do we bomb Sharon for his negation of Palestinian rights? Weren't we on Saddam's side when he was at his worst? (I am exempting the frantic and discredited few who think or suggest that George W. Bush fixed up the attacks to inflate the military budget and abolish the Constitution.) But however compromised and shameful the American starting point was—and I believe I could make this point stick with greater venom and better evidence than most people can muster—the above point remains untouched. The United States finds itself at war with the forces of reaction.

Do I have to demonstrate this? The Taliban's annihilation of music and culture? The enslavement of women? The massacre of Shiite Muslims in Afghanistan? Or what about the latest boast of al-Qaida—that the bomb in Bali, massacring so many Australian holidaymakers, was a deliberate revenge for Australia's belated help in securing independence for East Timor? (Never forget that the Muslim fundamentalists are not against "empire." They fight proudly for the restoration of their own lost caliphate.) To these people, the concept of a civilian casualty is meaningless if the civilian is an unbeliever or a heretic.

Confronted with such a foe—which gladly murders Algerians and Egyptians and Palestinians if they have any doubts about the true faith, or if they happen to be standing in the wrong place at the wrong time, or if they happen to be female—exactly what role does a "peace movement" have to play? A year or so ago, the peace movement was saying that Afghanistan could not even be approached without risking the undying enmity of the Muslim world; that the Taliban could not be bombed during Ramadan; that a humanitarian disaster would occur if the Islamic ultra-fanatics were confronted in their own lairs. Now we have an imperfect but recovering Afghanistan, with its population increased by almost two million returned refugees. Have you ever seen or heard any of those smart-ass critics and cynics make a self-criticism? Or recant?

To the contrary, the same critics and cynics are now lining up to say, "Hands off Saddam Hussein," and to make almost the same doom-laden predictions. The line that connects Afghanistan to Iraq is not a straight one by any means. But the oblique connection is ignored by the potluck peaceniks, and one can be sure (judging by their past form) that it would be ignored even if it were as direct as the connection between al-Qaida and the Taliban. Saddam Hussein denounced the removal of the Sunni Muslim–murdering Slobodan Milosevic, and also denounced the removal of the Shiite-murdering Taliban.

Reactionaries have a tendency to stick together (and I don't mean "guilt by association" here. I mean *guilt*). If the counsel of the peaceniks had been followed, Kuwait would today be the nineteenth province of Iraq (and based on his own recently produced evidence, Saddam Hussein would have acquired nuclear weapons). Moreover, Bosnia would be a trampled and cleansed province of Greater Serbia, Kosovo would have been emptied of most of its inhabitants, and the Taliban would still be in power in Afghanistan. Yet nothing seems to disturb the contented air of moral superiority that surrounds those who intone slogans of the peace movement.

There are at least three well-established reasons to favor what is euphemistically termed "regime change" in Iraq. The first is the flouting by Saddam Hussein of every known law on genocide and human rights, which is why the Senate—at the urging of Bill Clinton—passed the Iraq Liberation Act unanimously before George W. Bush had even been nominated. The second is the persistent effort by Saddam's dictatorship to acquire the weapons of genocide: an effort that can and should be thwarted and that was condemned by the United Nations before George W. Bush was even governor of Texas. The third is the continuous involvement by the Iraqi secret police in the international underworld of terror and destabilization. I could write a separate essay on the evidence for this; at the moment I'll just say that it's extremely rash for anybody to discount the evidence that we already possess. (And I shall add that any peace movement that even pretends to care for human rights will be very shaken by what will be uncovered when the Saddam Hussein regime falls. Prisons, mass graves, weapon sites . . . just you wait.)

None of these things on their own need necessarily make a case for an intervention, but taken together—and taken with the permanent threat posed by Saddam Hussein to the oilfields of the region—they add up fairly convincingly. Have you, or your friends, recently employed the slogan "No War for Oil"? If so, did you listen to what you were saying? Do you mean that oil isn't worth fighting for, or that oil resources aren't worth protecting? Do you recall that Saddam Hussein ignited the oilfields of Kuwait when he was in retreat, and flooded the local waterways with fire and pollution? (Should I patronize the potluckistas, and ask them to look up the pictures of poisoned birds and marine animals from that year?) Are you indifferent to the possibility that such a man might be able to irradiate the oilfields next time? *Of course* it's about oil, stupid.

To say that he might also do all these terrible things if attacked or threatened is to miss the point. Last time he did this, or massacred the Iraqi and Kurdish populations, he was withdrawing his forces under an international guarantee. The Iraqi and Kurdish peoples are now, by every measure we have or know, determined to be rid of him. And the hope, which is perhaps a slim one but very much sturdier than other hopes, is that the next Iraqi regime will be better and safer, not just from our point of view but from the points of view of the Iraqi and Kurdish peoples. The sanctions policy, which was probably always hopeless, is now quite indefensible. If lifted, it would only have allowed Saddam's oligarchy to reequip. But once imposed, it was immoral and punitive without the objective of regime change. Choose. By the way, and while we are choosing, if you really don't want war, you should call for the lifting of the no-fly zones over northern and southern Iraq. These have been war measures since 1991.

What would the lifting of the no-fly zones mean for the people who live under them? I recently sat down with my old friend Dr. Barham Salih, who is the elected prime minister of one sector of Iraqi Kurdistan. Neither he nor his electorate could be mentioned if it were not for the no-fly zones imposed—as a result of democratic

protest in the West—at the end of the last Gulf War. In his area of
Iraq, regime change has already occurred. There are dozens of newspapers, numerous radio and TV channels, satellite dishes, Internet
cafes. Four female judges have been appointed. Almost half the students at the University of Suleimaniyah are women. And a pro-al-
Qaida group, recently transferred from Afghanistan, is trying to
assassinate the Kurdish leadership and nearly killed my dear friend
Barham just the other day. . . . Now, why would this gang want to
make that particular murder its first priority?

Before you face that question, consider this. Dr. Salih has been
through some tough moments in his time. Most of the massacres and
betrayals of the Kurdish people of Iraq took place with American support or connivance. But the Kurds have pressed ahead with regime
change in any case. Surely a peace movement with any principles
should be demanding that the United States not abandon them again.
I like to think I could picture a mass picket in Seattle, offering soli-
darity with Kurdistan against a government of fascistic repression,
and opposing any attempt to sell out the Kurds for reasons of re-
alpolitik. Instead, there is a self-satisfied isolationism to be found,
which seems to desire mainly a quiet life for Americans. The option
of that quiet life disappeared a while back, and it's only coincidence
that for me it vanished in Seattle. The United States is now at war
with the forces of reaction, and nobody is entitled to view this battle
as a spectator. The Union under Lincoln wasn't wholeheartedly
against slavery. The USA under Roosevelt had its own selfish agenda
even while combating Hitler and Hirohito. The hot-and-cold war
against Stalinism wasn't exactly free of blemish and stain. How much
this latest crisis turns into an even tougher war with reaction, at home
or abroad, could depend partly upon those who currently think that
it is either possible or desirable to remain neutral. I say "could," even
though the chance has already been shamefully missed. But a mere
potluck abstention will be remembered only with pity and scorn.

"Cowboy"

BUSH CHALLENGED BY BOVINES.

January 27, 2003

To be reading the European press or visiting a European capital these days is to witness a strenuous competition. The competition, which is easy to enter but not at all easy to win, is to see how many times a person can get the word "cowboy" into an article or a speech. In normal times, an editor would probably limit the usage automatically, if only to avoid the vulgarity of repetition, but this quotidian rule is being relaxed these days. The term can appear any number of times as long as it is affixed to the proper name Bush.

On its own, the word "cowboy" is not particularly opprobrious. It means a ranch hand or cattle driver, almost by definition a mounted one, herding the steers in the general direction of Cheyenne and thus providing protein on the hoof. The job calls for toughness and has little appeal to the sentimental. A typical cowboy would be laconic, patient, somewhat fatalistic, and prone to spend his wages on brawling and loose gallantry. His first duty is to cattle, and he has to have an eye for weather. Unpolished, but in his way invaluable. A rough job but someone's got to do it. And so forth.

The old children's game of cowboys and Indians summarizes the association of the cowboy with the frontier and with the wars on the plains and ranges against the indigenous tribes. Actually, the cutting-edge work here was done with cavalry sabers, pox blankets, repeating rifles, and other weapons of routine destruction. Yet the word "cavalryman" is as indissoluble from the concept of chivalry as the word "cowboy" is from the notion of the uncouth.

Still a third implication is that of the lone horseman, up against the world with nothing more than his six-shooter and steed and lariat. He might be a stickup artist and the terror of the stagecoach industry, or he might be a solitary fighter for justice and vindicator of the rights of defenseless females. Henry Kissinger never quite recovered from the heartless mirth he attracted when he told Oriana Fallaci that Americans identified with men like himself—the solitary, gaunt hero astride a white horse (as opposed to the corpulent opportunist academic leaking to the press aboard a taxpayer-funded shuttle).

In England, "cowboy" is often used dismissively to describe a fly-by-night business or a shady or gamey entrepreneur, as well as anybody who, while making more noise and more claims than are good for him, is flaky when it comes to delivering the goods.

Finally, though Wyoming and Montana and other states are rich in lore, the word "cowboy" has a special relationship with the state of Texas, its lone star logo, and the name of its Dallas football team. (The laureate of the state and its cattle drives, Larry McMurtry, is oddly enough not considered by right-thinking people to be a hayseed or a gunslinger.) President Bush has played to this strength, if it is a strength, at least three times that I can think of. The first was when he admitted to having been a bit of a cowboy in his youth, in both personal and business terms. The second was when he called for the apprehension of Osama bin Laden and made a point of stressing the old Wanted poster words: "Dead or Alive." The third was when he was asked about the murder of an Arab American in Texas after September 11 and remarked rather ominously that the perpetrator had "picked the wrong state" in which to commit this outrage. One could almost see the noose snaking over the limb of the tree. . . .

Boiled down, then, the use of the word "cowboy" expresses a fixed attitude and an expectation, on the part of non-Texans, about people from Texas. It's a competition between a clichéd mentality (which would of course never dream of regarding itself as clichéd) and a cliché itself. How well—apart from some "with us or with the terrorists" rhetoric—does the president fit the stereotype?

To have had three planeloads of kidnapped civilians crashed into urban centers might have brought out a touch of the cowboy even in Adlai Stevenson. But Bush waited almost five weeks before launching any sort of retaliatory strike. And we have impressive agreement among all sources to the effect that he spent much of that time in consultation. A cowboy surely would have wanted to do something dramatic and impulsive (such as to blow up at least an aspirin factory in Sudan) in order to beat the chest and show he wasn't to be messed with. But it turns out that refined Parisians are keener on such "unilateral" gestures—putting a bomb onboard the *Rainbow Warrior*, invading Rwanda on the side of the killers, dispatching French troops to the Ivory Coast without a by-your-leave, building a reactor for Saddam Hussein, and all the rest of it.

In the present case of Iraq, a cowboy would have overruled the numerous wimps and fainthearts who he had somehow appointed to his administration and would have evinced loud scorn for the assemblage of sissies and toadies who compose the majority of the United Nations. Instead, Bush has rejoined UNESCO, paid most of the U.S. dues to the United Nations, and returned repeatedly to the podium of the organization in order to recall it to its responsibility for existing resolutions. While every amateur expert knows that weather conditions for an intervention in the Gulf will start to turn adverse by the end of next month, he has extended deadline after deadline. He has not commented on the eagerness of the media to print every injunction of caution and misgiving from State Department sources. The Saudis don't want the United States to use the base it built for the protection of "the Kingdom"? Very well, build another one in a state that welcomes the idea. Do the Turks and Jordanians want to have their palms greased before discovering what principles may be at stake? Greased they will be. In a way, this can be described as "a drive to war." But only in a way. It would be as well described as a decided insistence that confrontation with Saddam Hussein is inevitable—a proposition that is relatively hard to dispute from any standpoint. It's true that Bush was somewhat brusque with Chancellor Gerhard Schröder, but then Schröder is a man so sensitive that he sought an injunction against a London newspaper for printing speculation about his hair color and his notoriously volatile domestic life. What we are really seeing, in this and other tantrums, is not a Texan cowboy on the loose but the even less elevating spectacle of European elites having a cow.

"Recruitment"

WILL AN IRAQ WAR MAKE OUR AL-QAIDA PROBLEM WORSE? NOT LIKELY.

February 5, 2003

There is a parody of the old Uncle Sam "I Want YOU" recruiting poster in circulation. It shows Osama bin Laden in the Uncle Sam finger-pointing pose, proclaiming that he wants us to invade Iraq and thus generate massive infusions of young and eager talent to his ranks. In different verbal and cartoon forms, this thought has become part of the standard repertoire of those who take the regime-preservation or regime-prolongation view of Iraq.

Before examining the argument—if it is an argument—one might observe that these are often the same people who scoff at any connection between Saddam Hussein and al-Qaida, and who furthermore are the most critical of the war on al-Qaida and the Taliban. So, it might be noted that for this purpose at least, they take as a given what they otherwise doubt. Perhaps this is progress, even if unacknowledged. (When they say that Iraq is a "distraction," do please remember to ask them: "Distraction from what?" Then ask how keen they are on the battle against bin Laden.)

It is certainly curious, also, to notice that whether or not Saddam has given succor to al-Qaida, the bin Ladenist forces around the world have identified his cause with their own. In Kurdistan they fight, at least "objectively," on Saddam's side. In their propaganda, they speak absurdly of an intervention against Saddam as "an attack on a Muslim country," as if regime change could alter the confessional makeup of Iraq (which incidentally has many non-Muslims and Christians and used to have an immense Jewish population). But why should one suppose that Saddam's defeat would increase the appeal of al-Qaida and, even if we knew this to be true in advance, why should it make any difference?

Let me cite two of bin Laden's pronouncements. After the slaughter of Australian holidaymakers in Bali a few months ago, a statement was issued by al-Qaida that justified the mass murder on the grounds that Australian troops had assisted in East Timor's transition to independence. Bin Laden had many times venomously criticized the Australian involvement before September 11, so whether he is dead or alive the point is made: The Aussies brought this on themselves by helping a mainly Christian minority regain its independence from a mainly Muslim state. No doubt this same thought helped to swell the ranks of al-Qaida in Indonesia itself, where Islam sometimes makes a good fit with local chauvinism. The conclusion would appear to be this: The wise course would have been to leave the East Timorese to the tender mercies of the Indonesian oligarchy, since to involve oneself on their side was to risk bin Laden's ire. Is this what the recruiting-poster peddlers really want us to conclude?

In a sermon to his troops before September 11, and on many other occasions that we have on tape, bin Laden told them that beating the Soviet Union in Afghanistan had been the hard part. The destruction of the other superpower, he asserted, would be easy. America was soft and corrupt and sunk in luxury, controlled by venal Jews. It was so weak and decadent that it had run away from Somalia. It would not risk its own forces and could not face the idea of taking casualties. If you care for the evidence then, you might note that bin Laden recruits on the basis that the United States will *not* fight. (Admittedly he contradicts himself on this, sometimes referring to it as an unsleeping aggressor. But then, so do those who claim to interpret his wishes.) Still, if the administration were suddenly to decide that the risk of intervention in Iraq was too great, after all this preparation, then we could be sure that bin Laden's recruiting sergeants would make this cowardice and weakness a central point in their propaganda appeal.

In the early stages of the fighting in Afghanistan after September 11, I remember reading many peacenik arguments that the United States was playing into bin Laden's hands and doing exactly what he wanted. (Noam Chomsky made a particular point of this; others added that to kill bin Laden would cause thousands of new bin Ladens to spring up in his stead.) I have never seen it argued since that al-Qaida got what it wanted out of the Afghan operation. It lost its only host government, it had to abandon its safe houses in Kabul and Kandahar, it took an enormous number of casualties and had to flee ignominiously, it saw hundreds more of its cadres taken to Guantanamo Bay, and it may very well have left its charismatic leader somewhere under a rock. If this was all part of God's design, then he may well not be on their side. Moreover, it strikes me that Osama bin Laden himself is a one-of-a-kind sort of guy, unlikely to clone widely.

But what if he *was* able to reproduce himself in this way? Would this alchemy make him less of an enemy? Would it remove the obligation to defend civil society from theocratic nihilism? The proponents of the "recruitment" hypothesis are unclear on this point, but then—they are unclear on the whole point to begin with.

It seems obvious that there are those in the Muslim world who dislike or suspect the United States for what it does or does not do, and those who hate it for its very existence. The task of statecraft is to make this distinction and also to work hard and intelligently to make it wider. But to argue that nothing can be done lest it incur the displeasure of the second group is to surrender without a fight, *and then to get a fight anyway*. American support for elections and for women's rights would infuriate the second group just as much as American action against Saddam. There is, to put it very mildly, no pleasing some people. Nor should there be. Self-respect as well as sound strategy demands that we make the enemy worry what we will do, and not waste away worrying what he may think of us.

The Rat That Roared

ON FRANCE, THE FRENCH, CHIRAC, AND
THE DIFFERENCE BETWEEN THEM.

February 6, 2003

To say that the history of human emancipation would be incomplete without the French would be to commit a fatal understatement. The Encyclopedists, the proclaimers of Les Droites de l'Homme, the generous ally of the American Revolution . . . the spark of 1789 and 1848 and 1871, can be found all the way from the first political measure to abolish slavery, through Victor Hugo, Emile Zola, and Jean Jaurès to the gallantry of Jean Moulin and the *maquis* resistance. French ideas and French heroes have animated the struggle for liberty throughout modern times.

There is of course another France—the France of Petain and Poujade and Vichy and of the filthy colonial tactics pursued in Algeria and Indochina. Sometimes the United States has been in excellent harmony with the first France—as when Thomas Paine was given the key of the Bastille to bring to Washington, and as when Lafayette and Rochambeau made France the "oldest ally." Sometimes American policy has been inferior to that of many French people—one might instance Roosevelt's detestation of de Gaulle. The Eisenhower-Dulles administration encouraged the French in a course of folly in Vietnam, and went so far as to inherit it. Kennedy showed a guarded sympathy for Algerian independence, at a time when France was too arrogant to listen to his advice. So it goes. Lord Palmerston was probably right when he said that a nation can have no permanent allies, only permanent interests. It is not to be expected that any proud, historic country can be automatically counted "in."

However, the conduct of Jacques Chirac can hardly be analyzed in these terms. Here is a man who had to run for reelection last year partly in order to preserve his immunity from prosecution, on charges of corruption that were grave. Here is a man who helped Saddam Hussein build a nuclear reactor and who knew very well what he wanted it for. Here is a man at the head of France who is, in effect, openly for sale. He puts me in mind of the banker in Flaubert's *L'Education sentimentale:* a man so habituated to corruption that he would happily pay for the pleasure of selling himself.

Here, also, is a positive monster of conceit. He and his foreign minister, Dominique de Villepin, have unctuously said that "force is always the last resort." *Vraiment?* This was not the view of the French establishment when troops were sent to Rwanda to try and rescue the client regime that had just unleashed ethnocide against the Tutsi. It is not, one presumes, the view of the French generals who currently treat the people and nation of Cote d'Ivoire as their fief. It was not the view of those who ordered the destruction of an unarmed ship, the *Rainbow Warrior,* as it lay at anchor in a New Zealand harbor after protesting the French official practice of conducting atmospheric nuclear tests in the Pacific. (I am aware that some of these outrages were conducted when the French Socialist Party was in power, but in no case did Mr. Chirac express anything other than patriotic enthusiasm. If there is a truly "unilateralist" government on the Security Council, it is France.)

We are all aware of the fact that French companies and the French state are owed immense sums of money by Saddam Hussein. We all very much hope that no private gifts to any French political figures have been made by the Iraqi Baath Party, even though such scruple on either side would be anomalous to say the very least. Is it possible that there is any more to it than that? The future government in Baghdad may very well not consider itself responsible for paying Saddam's debts. Does this alone condition the Chirac response to a *fin de regime* in Iraq?

Alas, no. Recent days brought tidings of an official invitation to Paris, for Robert Mugabe. The president-for-life of Zimbabwe may have many charms, but spare cash is not among them. His treasury is as empty as the stomachs of his people. No, when the plumed parade brings Mugabe up the Champs-Elysées, the only satisfaction for Mr.

Chirac will be the sound of a petty slap in the face to Tony Blair, who has recently tried to abridge Mugabe's freedom to travel. Thus we are forced to think that French diplomacy, as well as being for sale or for hire, is chiefly preoccupied with extracting advantage and prestige from the difficulties of its allies.

This can and should be distinguished from the policy of Germany. Berlin does not have a neutralist constitution, like Japan or Switzerland. But it has a strong presumption against military intervention outside its own border, and Herr Schröder, however cheaply he plays this card, is still playing a hand one may respect. One does not find German statesmen positively encouraging the delinquents of the globe, in order to reap opportunist advantages and to excite local chauvinism.

Mr. Chirac's party is "Gaullist." Charles de Gaulle had a colossal ego, but he felt himself compelled at a crucial moment to represent *une certaine idée de la France*, at a time when that nation had been betrayed into serfdom and shame by its political and military establishment. He was later adroit in extracting his country from its vicious policy in North Africa, and gave good advice to the United States about avoiding the same blunder in Indochina. His concern for French glory and tradition sometimes led him into error, as with his bombastic statements about "Quebec libre." But—and this is disclosed in a fine study of the man, *À demain de Gaulle*, by the former French leftist Regis Debray—he always refused to take seriously the claims of the Soviet Union to own Poland and Hungary and the Czech lands and Eastern Germany. He didn't believe it would or could last: He had a sense of history.

To the permanent interests of France, he insisted on attaching *une certaine idée de la liberté* as well. He would have nodded approvingly at Vaclav Havel's statement—his last as Czech president—speaking boldly about the rights of the people of Iraq. And one likes to think that he would have had a fine contempt for his pygmy successor, the vain and posturing and venal man who, attempting to act the part of a balding Joan of Arc in drag, is making France into the abject procurer for Saddam. This is a case of the rat that tried to roar.

Inspecting "Inspections"

THE UNITED NATIONS IS STILL PLAYING SADDAM'S GAME.

February 13, 2003

Now that Osama bin Laden, or at any rate his organization, has called upon the forces of "jihad" to rally to the side of Saddam (and thus incidentally negated the idea that an intervention in Iraq would be a distraction from the war on terror), the time may have come for a brisk cleanup in our war terminology. No doubt new terms will soon be in play, but here is a wrap-up on the old ones.

"Material breach" and "inspections": Up until now, these expressions have regularly been employed in the wrong order. The Saddam Hussein regime has been, since 1992, in a continuous state of material breach of all its obligations to disarm. It was for this reason that a new resolution was passed by the Security Council of the United Nations, demanding that the decade-long breach be repaired. One has not yet run into anybody who believes that Saddam made any attempt to comply with the terms of the resolution, which indeed he did not. But one does hear the platonic theory that he might come into compliance, if only given more time. He happens to want more time for quite other reasons, so Hans Blix's disclosure that he might be undergoing "a change of heart" is an especially touching one.

Faced with all these material breaches, including conclusive evidence that the Iraqi authorities know when they are coming and where, the inspectors have to admit that they have become the objects of inspection rather than the conductors of it. In fact, it seems glaringly apparent to me that their ranks have been infiltrated, or suborned, or both. I know of at least one incontrovertible case where a senior inspector was offered a huge bribe by Tariq Aziz himself: The man in question refused the money, but perhaps not everybody did. Those who are calling for more time in this process should be aware that they are calling for more time for Saddam's people to complete their humiliation and subversion of the inspectors.

Colin Powell, who has been getting good press for getting good press (the highest honor that American culture can bestow), can be faulted for at least one and perhaps two of his performances. The first was the welcome he gave to the idea of a safe haven for Saddam Hussein, thus greatly weakening the moral basis for the claim of regime change. The second, arguably, was when he took his classified evidence and presented it to the United Nations. Paradoxically, this triumphant piece of public relations undermined the authority of the unanimous Security Council resolution it was designed to invoke. The resolution places the onus squarely on Iraq to prove that it has complied. There is no mention in the resolution of any requirement for the international community to furnish more evidence. Inspection is the term of art employed to describe the monitoring of compliance, not the unearthing of empirical proofs. As it happens, more empirical proofs have been unearthed, but no *investigation*, in the strict sense, has been carried out. If the United Nations was to call for an investigation of Iraq's arsenal, complete with inventory and accounting, it would logically have to call for the dispatch of armed peacekeepers, at the very least, in order to ensure access. Such a job could never be carried out by a small posse of civilians. And, given the square mileage of Iraq, the number of those armed peacekeepers would have to be pretty high.

This would not be an invasion by most definitions, but it would very much resemble an occupation. And that raises the question of the most central of all the fighting words, "War." Are we in fact talking about going to "war" at all? During the 1956 Anglo-French-Israeli attack upon Egypt, the preposterous British prime minister, Sir Anthony Eden, told Parliament that "we are not at war with Egypt. We are in a state of armed conflict." This was an obvious attempt to deny reality at a time when the Soviet Union, moreover, was threatening to intervene on Egypt's side.

But is it frivolous to ask whether the use of force in Iraq amounts to war in, say, the Vietnam sense of the term? "Stop the war before it starts" was the rather fatuous slogan of the peaceniks in the case of Afghanistan in 2001, and their plaintive slogan was echoed in reality because the "war" *was* over almost before it had begun. A war involves a minimum of two nations deploying their armed forces against each other: This could be only a technically apt description of hostilities as between the United States and its allies and the private army of Saddam Hussein. It would be just as accurate to say, "No quarrel with Saddam Hussein," as it would be to say, "No war on Iraq." And it might not be a euphemism to describe the impending event as the forcible removal of a hostile regime. It would certainly be at least as accurate as a description of the political objective.

This may seem like giving a hostage to fortune, but Saddam Hussein's armed forces mainly ran away or surrendered last time, and his air force had to be lent to Iran (which failed to return it), and there has been considerable degeneration in the morale and equipment of these forces since. The best that can be said of the Iraqi army is that it has not recently lost a war against its own civilians. Meanwhile, the evolution of PGMs—precision-guided mu nitions—makes it rational to hope that this distinction between combatant and computer can be observed on our side.

"Drumbeat"

BUSH RUSHING TO WAR? NONSENSE.

February 24, 2003

When George W. Bush was running for president, he campaigned energetically against Al Gore by objecting to the idea of "nation-building" (and, incidentally, to the Clinton-era practice of employing "secret evidence" in trials of suspected terrorists). After taking office, he opened an early discussion on the possibility of lifting Iraqi sanctions, which had obviously begun to suffer from diminishing returns. He even considered reviewing the no-fly zones that, for a wearisome decade or so, had placed an Anglo-American protective shield over the Kurdish and Shiite zones of Saddam's awful dominion.

In all of these respects, Bush was giving a sympathetic ear to a group of oilmen and generals, the first of whom did not like to see Iraqi oil being traded only with other countries, and the second of whom did not care to risk their sophisticated aircraft on drab, routine missions. Within his Cabinet and elsewhere in his administration, the president included a number of people who still believed that his father had been right, in 1991, to evacuate Iraq while leaving the Saddam Hussein regime in place. (Of this group, as far as I know, George Bush Sr. remains a dues-paying member, as do Brent Scowcroft and Lawrence Eagleburger. Only Vice President Dick Cheney, of the original team, is understood to have changed his mind—and that could well be for reasons of loyalty.)

Some "drumbeat." Some "drive to war." Since September 11, 2001, the Bush administration has:

1. Been to both houses of Congress in order to secure a warrant for intervention.

2. Rejoined UNESCO after two decades or so of American absence from the organization, and has agreed to pay most of the outstanding American back-dues to the U.N. itself. (Jan Kavan of the Czech Republic, this year's chairman of the U.N. General Assembly and no friend to the Bush doctrine, has said that he never believed that it would be this administration that decided to rejoin UNESCO.)

3. Been to the United Nations repeatedly to make the case; once to get a 15–0 Security Council resolution that contained the terms of its own enforcement; once to illustrate Iraqi noncompliance; and again to prepare a second resolution. It could reasonably be argued that under the terms of the first resolution it was not required to take the latter two steps.

Meanwhile, it is notorious that conditions for desert fighting decay, in point of strategic advantage to the Coalition, with every day that lengthens February into March. It must also be obvious that Saddam Hussein's goons have been put on notice to prepare their usual tactic of warfare against civilians and of sabotage against resources.

I caught Senator Hillary Clinton on some show from Albany, New York, where she said, with a knowing intonation, that obviously there were people in the Bush administration who had "an old score" to settle with Saddam Hussein. Many in the audience nodded appreciatively, as if being initiated into the secret of a grudge match. There are indeed people in the administration who never shared the prevailing Republican view that the last Gulf War was ended on acceptable or durable terms. But in eight of the intervening years Senator Clinton's husband was president of the United States, and it can hardly have escaped her notice that he called several times for the forcible disarmament of Saddam Hussein, stated roundly that Saddam pursued the acquisition of weapons of genocide only in order to use them, bombed Iraq for its part in a murder attempt on a former president, urged the passage of the Iraq Liberation Act (which carried the Senate nem con), and bombed Iraq again during every day of his own impeachment trial in the same deliberative body. True, he didn't always consult the United Nations so painstakingly. But then, nor was he confronted by a "peace" movement filling the streets and calling him an addict of aggression.

If there has been a drumbeat, then, it has been pounding itself out and rat-a-tat-tatting away for a very considerable time. Those who call for more time—for inspections or what have you—are acting as if the confrontation with Saddam Hussein began only a few months ago, as if he did not seek such a confrontation, and as if it were avoidable. These are all different versions of the same elementary mistake.

Saddam Hussein could have bought his regime a fresh lease on its ghastly life if he had been even slightly willing to "make nice," and the United States could have lowered its muzzle deep into Iraqi oil wells on the same unspoken understanding. It is even possible that at the last moment Saddam will try the options of self-preservation that his fans believe he both possesses and understands. There would be those, some of them in high positions in Washington, who would be willing to dump the Iraqi opposition and the Kurds on just this wager. (It's barely possible to imagine anything more shameful, but those who hope for such outcomes must be prepared to live with what they desire.) However, those who believe that the only way for America to get access to Iraqi oil is to take the chances of conflict and perhaps occupation have not even bothered to study the history of the region and can't be expected to start now.

But, reply those in the peace camp, weren't the troops already dispatched and the bases readied? Yes, they were, as they had been before. Do you wish they hadn't been? That could entail the always quite possible implosion of an already deeply traumatized Iraq, with perhaps opportunistic interventions from neighboring states and civil strife within Iraq itself. (The very dread consequences, indeed, which the antiwar movement somehow believes can only arise from a policy of regime change.) Now, at any rate, the forces that can prevent the sabotage of the oilfields and soften the meltdown of the state are within range. Do those who want a second resolution also propose to start such a complex buildup and deployment only on the day after the resolution passes? (They do, of course, which is what shows their culpable lack of seriousness.) Even the jackal Jacques Chirac has more sense than this: His only aircraft carrier is already in the Gulf and within reach in case he wants to switch sides.

Suppose it was the other way about (as it was in Bosnia and Kosovo and as one wishes it had not been with Rwanda). Suppose that the majority of European states or U.N. members urgently desired swift action, while the U.S. administration preferred to wait and see. To whom, in any event, would the task of intervention actually be delegated? The question answers itself, and it exposes the "drumbeat" and "drive" talk as idle chatter. Ask any Iraqi dissident and he or she will tell you what you already know (and what some antiwar propaganda actually states, without appreciating its own implications): Washington has been too patient with Saddam Hussein and for far too long.

Not Talking Turkey

AN ALLY WE'RE BETTER OFF WITHOUT.

March 4, 2003

The slander of the Iraqi and Kurdish opposition, and of their friends, as little better than puppets of the Bush administration is an idea that is half alive in the minds of those who are knowingly trying to buy more time for Saddam Hussein. Every now and then, one gets a sneer about it. So, it's good to step aside from the everyday arguments with the regime preservers and point out that proxies and mercenaries seldom express themselves as forcefully and publicly as has the Iraqi opposition.

The first point of disagreement—about the role of American officers in the aftermath—is a matter of principle but still somewhat contingent since nobody can know in advance what conditions will be in the post-Baathist republic. Many of the supplies required for rebuilding may be deliverable, for example, only by military transports. Nonetheless, a strong presumption has been established against any uniformed tutelage; the Iraqi National Congress, the Shiite forces, and the Kurds have united forcefully on the issue of self-government.

A second point of dissent hardly admits of any negotiation at all. Turkey has no rights in any part of Iraq, and least of all does it have any right to involve itself in the Kurdish areas, emancipated for a dozen years from Saddam's rule, which adjoin its own borders. The Bush administration has been entirely too lenient with Ankara, not just on this point but on many related ones:

1. Kurdistan itself. It has taken decades for the Turkish state even to acknowledge that another people with a distinct language

and culture lives within its borders. It's sadly true that a Kurdish rebellion in southeastern Turkey was led by a Shining Path–type leader named Abdullah Ocalan (believe me: I interviewed him in Lebanon and found a Kurdish Pol Pot), but this in itself expresses the desperate conditions that obtain. Under steady civilian pressure from within and without, Turkish authorities are now prepared to concede on the Kurdish right to exist—principally because the European Union has insisted on the point. The time for Washington to make a statement about Kurdish rights in Turkey would be right about now. (We have only been waiting since Woodrow Wilson first murmured on the same point.)

2. Cyprus. If any regime in the world has collected a bigger sheaf of resolutions condemning its international behavior than the Iraqi one, it must be the Turks (followed perhaps by the Israelis).

Since 1974, Turkey has patrolled a line of forcible partition drawn by its own troops—the first alteration of the territory of another European state since 1945. It has expelled almost one-third of the original Greek inhabitants and further violated international law by importing settlers and colonists from the Anatolian mainland. It has been condemned for murder, rape, and theft by innumerable European court rulings. So abysmal are conditions in its sweatshop colony in northern Cyprus, policed by the notorious thug and proxy Rauf Denktash, that the majority of Turkish Cypriots have joined vast demonstrations calling for an end to his rule and a federal brotherhood with their Greek co-citizens. Turkey could not hang on to Cyprus for a day without vast tranches of American military aid that shield it from the real cost of the annexation. This aid should be cut off without any further shameful delay: It makes the United States an accomplice in a gross violation of international law and human rights.

3. Armenia. The destruction and dispossession of the Armenian people, in the first ethnocide of the twentieth century, is not the responsibility of Turkey's present-day elected government. Nonetheless, the Turkish authorities continue to disown any historical responsibility and even to deny that the massacres occurred at all. Repeated proposals in the U.S. Senate to observe a day for Armenian Americans (bravely sponsored for years by former senator Robert Dole) have been defeated by an alliance of defense contractors owed money by Turkey and an Israeli lobby that desires to avoid offending a "Muslim" ally. It is improbable that Turkey would cease its heavy consumption of American aid if the resolution passed: It is intolerable that aid should be granted as a collusion in such a denial.

A footnote: The Ottoman Empire employed many Kurdish mercenaries as shock troops in the killing of Armenians. I have interviewed Jalal Talabani of the Patriotic Union of Kurdistan and heard him offer an apology on the record for this blot: Kurds do not confess to crimes that they have not committed. Thus the moral element in one instance is, as one might expect, inseparably linked to the moral case in another.

It may be argued that, in order to shorten the period of hostilities with Saddam Hussein and minimize casualties, the Iraqi border should be secured from all directions. But the Turks do not propose to help guarantee this border or to protect those who live within it. Rather, they propose to cross the frontier for no better reason than to aggrandize themselves and to prolong the subjection of their own Kurdish population. This doesn't just disgrace the regime-change strategy. It actually destabilizes it. And it's humiliating to see the president begging and bribing the Turks to do the wrong thing and to see them in return reject his offer. He should take their ugly egotism and selfishness as a compliment to his policy, cut off their aid, leave them to put their own case to the European Union, and tell them to get out of Cyprus in the bargain. Then we could be surer that we were really "remaking" the region.

* * *

Addendum

The Turkish leadership makes play of the fact that there is a "Turkic" minority—usually known as the Turkmen—living in Iraqi Kurdistan. This claim is true, though the numbers and proportions are sometimes exaggerated, and the Turkmen have as much claim to recognition as any other of the numerous Iraqi minorities. However, the claim of Mother Turkey to be their protector and defender should be viewed—especially in the light of its opportunistic assertion—with the utmost suspicion.

It was on the pretext of a Turkish minority that Ankara seized more than a third of the territory of Cyprus during the course of two invasions in the summer of 1974. (The minority, in contrast to this undisguised landgrab, was 18 percent of the population.) This aggression, with its mass expulsion of Greek Cypriots, annexation of territory, importation of settlers, and theft of property, has been repeatedly and overwhelmingly condemned by the United Nations. As I pointed out, and as can be easily verified, the majority of Turkish Cypriots are now themselves in rebellion against the colonial conditions created by the occupier. So, there should be no confusion at all between the rights of the Turkmen and the imperial ambitions of the Turkish state. Those who care about a "northern front" for regime change demand instead that weapons be given to the Kurdish guerrilla and militia organizations, which have demonstrated an ability to fight Saddam and are quite ready to defend their autonomy against Turkish arrogance at the same time. In both causes and both cases, they ought to be supported. Might it not be nice if France and the European Union and others issued a strong denunciation in advance of any Turkish unilateralism? Here, too, is a cause that a serious "peace" movement might take up.

Pious Nonsense

THE UNHOLY "CHRISTIAN" CASE
AGAINST WAR.

March 10, 2003

An awful realization has been dawning upon the Bush White House: Christianity is a religion of peace. From every pulpit, an appalling ecumenicism is preached, which calls for "more time" at best and for a "hands off Saddam" line at worst. The papal envoy to Iraq, Cardinal Etchegaray, has told us that Saddam Hussein "is doing everything to avoid war." With the addition only of a qualifying "this" as its penultimate word, that statement would actually have the merit of being true. I think we can all agree that Saddam likes the status quo to be undisturbed by any violence that is not his own.

However, the strongly implied corollary was that "war," if it should come, would be a strictly American responsibility. How else to interpret the remarks of Cardinal Solano, secretary of state to the Vatican, who bleated: "We want to say to America: Is it worth it to you? Won't you have, afterwards, decades of hostility in the Islamic world?" This solicitude for the feelings of pro-Saddam Muslims—of whom the leading faction is constituted by al-Qaida—is new for Holy Mother Church. The pope himself met with Tariq Aziz, who has for many years been the Christian (actually Chaldean Catholic) face of an openly national-socialist party. On these and other grounds, Aziz had a friendly audience with his holiness before going to pose as a pacifist in St. Francis's old praying ground at Assisi. Tariq Aziz's son was recently sentenced to twenty years in an Iraqi jail by Saddam Hussein—an effective means of reminding Saddam's suave envoy who is boss. (He does that all the time, by the way.) The Holy Father really ought to have asked to hear Aziz's confession. But perhaps he couldn't spare the time for such an arduous undertaking.

One wonders what it would take for the Vatican to condemn Saddam's regime. Baathism consecrates an entire country to the worship of a single human being. Its dictator has mosques named after himself. I'm not the expert on piety, but isn't there something blasphemous about this from an Islamic as well as a Christian viewpoint? I suppose if Saddam came out for partial-birth abortions or the ordination of women or the acceptance of the homosexual lifestyle he might be hit with a condemnation of some sort. (One might have hoped to argue that his abuse of children would get him in hot water with the Vatican, too. But even that expectation now seems vain.)

In one way, the church's "peace at any price" policy is a historical improvement. The last instance I can find of Rome supporting a war was when it blessed General Franco's invasion of Spain, at the head of an army of Muslim mercenaries who were armed and trained by Hitler and Mussolini. And everybody knows of the Crusades, which were launched against Christian heretics as well as against Muslims and (invariably) the Jews. But one wonders how the theory of just war, largely evolved by Catholic intellectuals such as Augustine and Aquinas, ever managed to endorse the use of force. As applied these days, it appears to commit everybody but Saddam Hussein to an absolute renunciation of violence.

You could see this paradox demonstrated on the *New York Times* op-ed page, by Jimmy Carter: peanut czar, home-builder, Nobel laureate, and Baptist big mouth. Reviewing just war precepts, our former president considered the obligation of weaponry to discriminate between combatants and noncombatants. He then asserted:

> *Extensive aerial bombardment, even with precise accuracy, inevitably results in "collateral damage." General Tommy R. Franks, commander of American forces in the Persian Gulf, has expressed concern about many of the military targets being near hospitals, schools, mosques and private homes.*

Where to begin? Under that condition, there are no circumstances in which a military intervention in Iraq could be justified. Someone could get killed. Then again, a man so deeply committed to Habitat for Humanity might ask what kind of habitat this is, where civilians are used as human shields, and weapons of poison and disease are concealed under places of worship. Last time, Saddam even seized hundreds of foreign nationals in Kuwait and prepared to put them between retribution and himself. (The funniest news of the week, incidentally, was the decision of the "human shield" volunteer activists to run away from Iraq. Most of them obviously didn't have the guts for it, but some of them, one hopes, had finally worked out what it was they were really shielding.)

Carter announced himself as "a Christian and as a president who was severely provoked by international crises." More accurate would have been "who provoked several severe international crises." It was the Carter administration that green-lighted, and later armed and aided, Saddam Hussein's distinctly unilateral invasion of Iran in 1979, an invasion that cost about a million and a half casualties, many of them civilian. I don't recall Carter being "provoked" by that at all. Incidentally, he describes the present American posture as "substantially unilateral," a piece of casuistry that wouldn't disgrace Cardinal Etchegaray himself.

Speaking of casuistry, Carter helpfully added that "American efforts to tie Iraq to the 9/11 terrorist attacks have been unconvincing." This might be narrowly true, with respect of the planning of the last attacks and given the use of the weak word "unconvincing." But the same day's *New York Times* carried a report with persuasive evidence of a substantial number of bin Ladenists on Iraqi soil. It's as hard to get into Iraq as it is to get out, and no Baathist official would make such a safe-haven decision without referring it to The Leader.

As a member of Atheists for Regime Change, a small but resilient outfit, I can't say that any of this pious euphemism, illogic, and moral cowardice distresses me. It shows yet again that there is a fixed gulf between religion and ethics. I hope it's borne in mind by the president, next time he wants to make a speech implying that God is on the side of the United States (and its godless Constitution). The leading experts in the supernatural, including also the Archbishop of Canterbury, many rabbis, most imams, and Bush's own United Methodists appear to agree that this is not so. The Almighty seems, if anything, to have smiled on Saddam Hussein for a quarter of a century. If we want to assure ourselves of a true "coalition of the willing," we might consider making a pact with the devil.

(Un)Intended Consequences

WHAT'S THE FUTURE IF WE *DON'T* ACT?

March 17, 2003

There has been a certain eeriness to the whole Iraq debate, from the moment of its current inception after September 11, 2001, right through the phony period of protracted legalism that has just drawn to a close. It was never really agreed, between the ostensibly contending parties, what the argument was "about." (Nor had it been in the preceding case of Kuwait in 1991: You may remember Secretary of State James Baker on that occasion exclaiming that the justification could be summarized in the one word "jobs.") Nobody has yet proposed that this is a job-creating war—though it may turn out to be—nor has anyone argued that it will be a job-losing one (though it might turn out to be that, too). The president bears his share of responsibility for this, for having made first one case and then another. So do the antiwar types, for picking up and discarding a series of straw arguments.

Conspicuous among the latter is the assertion that proponents of regime change have been *too* consistent. On every hand, I hear it darkly pointed out that several neoconservative theorists have wanted to get rid of Saddam Hussein for a very long time. Even before September 11! Even before the invasion of Kuwait! It's easy to look up the official papers and public essays in which Paul Wolfowitz, for example, has stressed the menace of Saddam Hussein since as far back as 1978. He has never deviated from this conviction. What could possibly be more sinister?

The consistency with which a view is held is of course no guarantee of that view's integrity. But it seems odd to blame Wolfowitz for having in effect been right all along. Nor, by his repeated hospitality and generosity to gangsters from Abu Nidal to Islamic Jihad and al-Qaida (in the latter instance most obviously after September 11, 2001), has Saddam Hussein done much to prove him wrong. So, the removal of this multifarious menace to his own population, to his neighbors, and to targets further afield would certainly be an "intended consequence" of a policy long meditated at least on some people's part.

What of the "unintended" consequences? By some bizarre convention, only those who favor action to resolve this long-running conflict are expected to foresee, or to take responsibility for, the future. But there's no evading the responsibility here, on either side. (I wouldn't want, for example, the responsibility of having argued for prolonging the life of a fascist regime.) But who can be expected to predict the future? The impossibility doesn't stop people from trying. Jimmy Carter, in 1991, wrote a public letter to Arab heads of state urging them to oppose the forcible eviction of Saddam Hussein from Kuwait. An American-led counterattack would, he instructed them, lead at once to massive rioting and disorder across the Islamic world. It would cause untold numbers of casualties. And it would lead to an increase in terrorism. Now Carter has said all this again in a much-noticed op-ed piece. He could even be right this time, but not for any reason or reasoning that he's been able to demonstrate.

As an experiment, let's take a Carter policy. As president, he encouraged Saddam Hussein to invade Iran in 1979 and assured him that the Khomeini regime would crumble swiftly. The long resulting war took at least a million and a half lives, setting what is perhaps a record for Baptist-based foreign policy and severely testing Carter's proclaimed view that war is a last resort. However, of these awful casualties, an enormous number were fervent Iranian "revolutionary guards," who were flung into battle as human waves. Not only did this rob Shiite fundamentalism of its most devoted volunteers, but it left Iran with a birth deficit. The ayatollahs then announced a policy of replenishment, financing Iranian mothers with special inducements and privileges if they would have large families. The resulting baby-boom generation is now entering its twenties and has, to all outward intents and purposes, rejected the idea of clerical rule. The "Iranian street" is, if anything, rather pro-American. How's that for an unintended or unforeseen consequence?

Or take another thought experiment, this time from one of Carter's lugubrious warnings. There are some smart people who have come to believe that the first bombing of the World Trade Center, in 1993, was in fact a terrorist revenge for Kuwait on Saddam Hussein's part. Ramzi Yusef, generally if boringly described as the "mastermind" of that and related plots—and the nephew of al-Qaida's apprehended Khalid Shaikh Mohammed—may have been an Iraqi agent operating with a Kuwaiti identity forged for him during Saddam's occupation of that country. One cannot be sure. But suppose that this *was* a terrorist counterstroke of the sort that is now so widely predicted to be in our future rather than our past. Would it have been better to have let Saddam Hussein keep Kuwait and continue work on what was (then) his nuclear capacity? That seems to be the insinuation of those who now argue that a proactive policy only makes our enemies more cross.

If consequences and consistency are to count in this argument, then they must count both ways. One cannot know the future, but one can make a reasoned judgment about the evident danger and instability of the status quo. Odd that the left should think that the status quo, in this area of all areas, is so worthy of preservation.

Giving Peace a Chance

THE WAR CRITICS WERE RIGHT—NOT IN THE WAY THEY EXPECTED.

April 9, 2003

So it turns out that all the slogans of the antiwar movement were right after all. And their demands were just. "No War on Iraq," they said—and there wasn't a war on Iraq. Indeed, there was barely a "war" at all. "No Blood for Oil," they cried, and the oil wealth of Iraq has been duly rescued from attempted sabotage with scarcely a drop spilled. Of the nine oil wells set ablaze by the few desperadoes who obeyed the order, only one is still burning and the rest have been capped and doused without casualties. "Stop the War" was the call. And the "war" is indeed stopping. That's not such a bad record. An earlier antiwar demand—"Give the Inspectors More Time"—was also very prescient and is also about to be fulfilled in exquisite detail.

So I'm glad to extend the hand of friendship to my former antagonists and to begin the long healing process. Perhaps one might start by meeting another of their demands and lifting the sanctions? Now that the inspectors are well and truly in, there's no further need for an embargo. I noticed that Kofi Annan announced in early April that the Iraqi people should be the ones to decide their own government and future. I don't mind that he never said this before: It's enough that he says it now.

What else? Oh yes, the Arab street did finally detonate, just as the peace movement said it would. You can see the Baghdad and Basra and Karbala streets filling up like anything, just by snapping on your television. And the confrontation with Saddam Hussein *did* lead to a surge in terrorism, with suicide bombers and a black-shirted youth movement answering his call. As could also have been predicted, those determined to die are now dead. We were told that Baghdad would become another Stalingrad—which it has. Just as in Stalingrad after 1956, all the statues and portraits of the heroic leader have been torn down.

Some other predictions, it is true, didn't fare so well. Saddam Hussein didn't manage to fire any poisons into Israel (where they would also have slaughtered the Palestinians), and the Israeli government didn't seize the chance to expel the population of the occupied territories. Nor did the Turks manage to annex Iraqi Kurdistan. Osama bin Laden, or one of his ghostwriters, did admittedly call for a jihad. But then, he always does that. Meanwhile, the Muslim world and its clerics seem decidedly undecided about whether Saddam really was a great Saladin after all. The Sunni Kurds and the Shiite slum dwellers, who fought against Saddam and who rebelled against him the first chance they got, would appear on the face of it to have as good a claim to be Muslim as anybody else.

But these are mere quibbles. We should celebrate our common ground as well as the gorgeous mosaic of our diversity. The next mass mobilization called by International ANSWER and the stop-the-war coalition is only a few days away. I already have my calendar ringed for the date. This time, I am really going to be there. It is not a time to keep silent. Let our voices be heard. All of this has been done in my name, and I feel like bearing witness.

Oleaginous

PEOPLE WHO PREFER SADDAM HUSSEIN TO HALLIBURTON.

April 18, 2003

In the waning days of the argument over whether to intervene in Iraq, I came to think that I could, with a 99 percent chance of being bang on target and inflicting no collateral damage, spot an obvious phony. At the meeting or the debate, the person concerned would get up and—without loss of time—announce that of course we'd all be better off without the bad guy Saddam Hussein. Having cleared his or her throat in this manner, the phony would go on to say what the *real* problem was (East Timor sometimes, or the imminent obliteration of tens of thousands of Baghdadi civilians, or Sharon's plan to expel all the inhabitants of the West Bank under cover of an American imperialist war).

None of the hysterical predictions came true, of course, but now I can't open a bulletin from the reactionary Right or the antiwar Left without being told that Iraq is already worse off without Saddam Hussein. My suspicion—that these people never meant what they affected to say—is thereby materialized. And how can we tell that Iraq is worse off? Because contracts for its reconstruction are being awarded to American corporations. Can that be right? In other words, of the three feasible alternatives (that the contracts go to American capitalists, or to some unspecified non-American capitalists, or that Iraqi oil production stays where it was), the supposed radicals appear to prefer the last of the three.

This view, which admittedly expresses a wider concern, can stand some examination. Let us, first, not forget what the preexisting sta-

tus quo involved. The Iraqi oil industry was until March 2003 a fief-
dom of the Baath Party. Its revenues were mysteriously apportioned
but went to the upkeep of a militaristic and dictatorial regime. Its
physical plant was much decayed, as a consequence of United Nations
sanctions. The "oil-for-food" program was exploited in the most cynical manner by members and clients of the palatial Saddam regime,
who used the semilegal trade to enrich themselves while starving and
neglecting the population. (By the way, now that sanctions can be
properly lifted, let us remember that their very imposition was opposed by the antiwar spokesmen, who would have scrapped them
without conditions even though they had been imposed by the sacro-
sanct majority of the U.N.) Meanwhile, vast contracts were awarded,
on the basis of obvious political favoritism, to Russian and French
consortia. At moments when the Baathist authorities felt themselves
insecure, they would threaten to set fire to the oil wells or—as in late
March—would actually ignite them.

In front of me is a copy of the *Arab Times*, published in Kuwait
City and picked up during my recent trip to the region. It gives a
matter-of-fact account of the state of affairs in the Rumaila field, as
of March 29, 2003. About ten oil wells were ablaze on that date: many
fewer than had at one time been feared or anticipated. (A large number of bombs and charges had been laid, but either the local officers
did not obey the order, or the order never came, or the fields were secured by British and American Special Forces too swiftly to allow the
planned sabotage to occur.)

At any rate, a burning well is a tough proposition and an uncapped
well—permitting a wholesale discharge—an even tougher one. The
situation was being handled by Boots and Coots, a fire-control company with an almost parodically American name that is based in Hous-
ton, Texas. Boots and Coots, which also worked in Kurdistan and
Kuwait after the much worse conflagrations of 1991, is subcontracted
for the task by Kellogg, Brown and Root (another name that Harold
Pinter might have coined for an American oil company), which is in
turn a subdivision of Halliburton. And Halliburton, which admittedly
sounds more British and tony than Boots and Coots, was once headed
by—cue mood music of sinister corporate skyscraper as the camera
pans up in the pretitle sequence—Vice President Dick Cheney. Thus
the Kuwaiti financial pages, reporting in mid-combat.

Well, if that doesn't give away the true motive for the war, I am sure that I don't know what does. Except that a moment's thought is enough to allow some further reflections. Unless the antiwar forces believe that Saddam's fires should be allowed to burn out of control indefinitely (and I would hate even to suspect them of anything so careless), they must presumably have an idea of which outfit should have gotten the contract *instead* of Boots and Coots. I think we can be sure that the contract would not have gone to some windmill-power concern run by Naomi Klein or the anti-Starbucks Seattle coalition, in the hope of just blowing out the flames, or of extinguishing them with Buddhist mantras—windy as those are. The number of real-world companies able to deliver such expertise is very limited. The chief one is American, and was personified for years by Red Adair and the movie version of his exploits (made by John Wayne himself!) entitled *Hellfighters*. The other main potential bidder, according to a learned recent letter in the London *Times*, is French. But would it not also be blood for oil to award the contract in that direction? After all, didn't the French habitually put profits in Iraq ahead of human rights and human life? More to the point, don't they still?

The main charge against Cheney and indeed Rumsfeld, after all, is that they used to be, not too hostile to Saddam, but too chummy with him. Too greedy for contracts and contacts. That was oil-based also, was it not? Why are the Saudis so opposed to regime change in Iraq if the fabled oil lobby is so much in favor of it? Could it be that oil always influences everybody's stance toward Iraq?

I want to be the first to agree that transparency in the administration and allocation of oil revenues is of the first importance. For example, there is a gigantic amount of money involved in the U.N.-administered oil-for-food program. Vast quantities of this surplus are still unspent, and are backed up somewhere within a complex bureaucracy. The Kurdish people, for example, are still waiting to see how much of their hard-won cash will be released for the rebuilding of their desolated homeland. Escrow isn't enough. All we know is that many U.N. officials are sitting contentedly on the transfers, and that the great undisclosed balance is held in a French bank. Here's a good cause for the humanitarians to take up, if they are willing to do some work and some digging instead of mouthing a few easy slogans.

If you are as persuaded of the materialist conception of history as (say) I am, then you owe it to yourself to study the dialectic and to avoid tautology. A theory that seems to explain everything is just as good at explaining nothing. In Guatemala in 1954, and in Iran at about the same time, and later in Chile in 1973, it is true that the United Fruit Company, and the Anglo-Iranian oil corporation, and Pepsi and ITT all influenced regime change too much. Sometimes, politics really was like a Bertolt Brecht script where the fat man in a top hat pays the bills and pulls all the strings. But in Iraq this proposed scenario is believed in only by the puerile. It's the baby-oil theory. It was for the sake of real oil and for the grim-faced Saudis that Saddam Hussein was kept as a favorite by Washington during the 1980s, and saved from overthrow in 1991. It was not for the sake of oil that the risky decision to cease this corrupt coexistence was made. But at least now the Iraqi people have a chance of controlling their own main re-source, and it will be our task to ensure that the funding and revenue are transparent instead of opaque. This couldn't have been left to the oil interests who ran the place until recently, and it couldn't even have been attempted if we'd listened to the peaceniks, who strike me now more than ever as . . . oleaginous.

* * *

Postscript

In early April I ran into Mayor Jerry Brown of Oakland, who had that day ordered his police department to stand firm. "Antiwar" pro-testors had tried to blockade and occupy the port of Oakland partly on the grounds that a local company had won a contract to help reopen the southern Iraqi port of Umm Qasr. Thus the peaceniks tried, in a moment of moral urgency for others if not for themselves, to choke off the only existing flow of humanitarian aid to Iraq. Nice work.

EPILOGUE
After the Fall ...

April 16, 2003

Why on earth do people keep saying that it's easy to be wise after the event? Few enterprises are as difficult and demanding as that (otherwise the work of the historian would be simplistic and one-dimensional). However, while taking care to avoid the consoling American damage-control cliché about "twenty-twenty hindsight," one may still attempt a moral and political balance sheet.

On the morning of April 9, 2003, the streets of Dearborn, Michigan, were *en fete*. Crowds of Iraqi-American exiles displayed the Stars and Stripes, honked horns, shouted praise for the United States and Britain, and defaced pictures of Saddam Hussein. Their action was a sort of echo and replay of what could be seen in Baghdad and especially in Fardus ("Paradise") Square in the center of the capital, where the crowd enlisted American know-how to pull down the colossus of Saddam Hussein and later to drag its severed head through the streets, showered in kicks and spittle. This in turn emulated an earlier British action in Basra, where one of the thousands of crude and imposing Saddam statues had been wrenched from its plinth by the Irish Guards. In some ways, the climactic scene in Baghdad was reminiscent of the most frequently evoked analogy: the fall of the Berlin Wall. But a more exact European comparison might have been the tearing of an immense Josef Stalin image from its statuesque podium in central Budapest in the fall of 1956. Only his big metal boots remained, forlorn and contemptible. (A photograph of these stumps once adorned the cover of the Marxist review *International Socialism*, a publication I served long ago in the capacity of literary editor. But that was before the Western Left became a status quo force, relativist and neutralist about totalitarian dictatorships.)

In some superficial ways, the jacquerie in Baghdad was picture perfect. The stone mount of the Saddam statue turned out to conceal some shoddy brickwork, which crumbled easily into filthy powder. But not all the metaphors were as apt as that. An American marine corporal took the opportunity to drape the flag of the United States over the face of the fallen Ozymandias. That would have been all very well in Dearborn, Michigan, but in Baghdad it transgressed an explicit standing order. However, the al-Jazeera network did not report this fine distinction in its coverage of the moment. Corporal Edward Chin, who defied discipline and protocol to perform this unscripted action, was a good story in himself. He was an ethnic Chinese volunteer for the marines, whose parents had fled the gruesome dictatorship in Burma—now Myanmar—in search of a new life in Brooklyn. The flag he brought along had been flying at the Pentagon on September 11, 2001, when a commandeered planeful of civilians had been smashed into a flank of the building. It was to turn out that perhaps 30,000 of the American fighting men and women in the Gulf region were only "green card" holders, whose papers of citizenship had not, like Corporal Chin's, come to them as a birthright, or at all. Many of these had names like Gutierrez and came from cities like Los Angeles and, if they were killed in action, received full citizenship retrospectively. Others, mustered into separate detachments, had names like Abdallah and had volunteered to return home to Iraq as soldiers and interpreters. These had recently been trained in special encampments in Hungary.

Choked-up feelings of emotion at liberation are the surest sign that a moment of disillusion and disappointment is at hand. The marvelous demolition of the Stalin statue in Budapest was followed by the brutal lynching of actual and suspected secret policemen and, in some quarters of the city, by a recrudescence of anti-Semitism directed at the many Jews in high Communist positions. This did not negate the grandeur of the Hungarian revolution, but it did somewhat disfigure it. The fall of the Bastille itself was a prelude to ochlocracy and worse. There was much less revenge killing, in Baghdad and Basra and Kirkuk in the first days, than I had sometimes feared there would be.

But then in my moments of deepest apprehension I had not expected to see the hysterical murder of Imam al-Khoie, that great Shia patriot and dissident exile, just outside the holy shrine to which he had loyally returned. And how could one be proud of the punctilious way in which the bombing had spared the cultural edifices of Baghdad (most reporters entering the city were amazed to see its undamaged look) when nobody had thought to put a guard on the National Museum, the library, and the Islamic archives.

Your own choice of a high moment, if I may invite it, from David Lean's *Lawrence of Arabia?* Let's agree to exempt the resplendent scene of flogging and implied rape, which is the cheapest kind of Orientalism. ("You're just Florence of Arabia," as a cynical producer once phrased it to Peter O'Toole.) That might leave us to choose between the bitter trek by hardened freedom fighters across the desert, the pitiless bombing of Arab tents by Ottoman aircraft, the sabotage of the Hijaz railway by guerrilla warriors, the orgiastic massacre of the retreating foe by Lawrence and his overenthusiastic volunteers, and the quagmire or quicksand that engulfs his young "friend" Daud. For me, though, the climax of the film has always been the anticlimax. Having taken Jerusalem and then Damascus, the Arab forces begin to quarrel and bicker, and to look with glittering annoyance upon their Western allies and patrons. Chaos, tribalism and egomania overwhelm the grand enterprise. In the movie, the British General Allenby just watches cynically as the revolt peters out. There is a scene where he clearly and deliberately gives the locals just enough time to pillage and loot, so as to wreck their own chances. And then the Arabs leave the city and fade back into the sand dunes, and out of history. What else could one expect?

In June 1976 I spent a while in the Iraqi National Museum in Baghdad, doing some amateur research on the legend of Gilgamesh for a friend who hoped to write an opera on the subject. My guide was a poised and polished man named Mazen al-Zahawi: a professional "minder" for the regime, it is true (he also took me to see the notorious assassin and saboteur Abu Nidal, then living openly as a guest of the Baath Party), but a fine companion for all that. He was partly Kurdish and wholly gay. He lived in the former Nazi German embassy residence near the Tigris—an elegant enough house—and invited me for dinner with a publisher friend of his who lived on a houseboat. There he told me that his favorite recreation was to improvise a Mesopotamian version of Wilde's *The Importance of Being Earnest*, with himself in the part of Lady Bracknell. Dear Mazen went on to become Saddam Hussein's interpreter, because of his superb English, and I wondered how long he'd survive. (Not all that long: He was tortured to death on a whim and then denounced for being a queer.) I mourn him terribly, along with many other brave and witty Iraqi and Kurdish friends. But I think he would rather have died himself than have seen the recent vandalizing and desecration of the museum, and the National Library. Is it profane to care as much for artifacts as for people? What are we defending when we talk about civilization?

It may seem like a small thing, even a trivial thing, but I spent an appreciable bit of my time in the early months of 2003 arguing just one point with people in Washington. Whatever you do about Iraq, or in Iraq, please don't give it the code name "Desert." Everything is wrong with that designation. This is not a land of dunes and camels, as Bush Senior's "Desert Storm" and Clinton's "Desert Fox" condescendingly implied. It is a highly evolved and complex society. It is the site of Babylon and Ur and Babel, and the womb of the founding myths of civilization. (*Gilgamesh* describes the building of a boat to survive a predicted flood.) Some of the very earliest Christian places are to be found there, and until 1948 there were more Jews in Baghdad than there were in Jerusalem. And our folklore doesn't come from the Brothers Grimm: It originates with Sinbad, Scheherazade, and Haroun al-Rashid.

One of the most vivid of these ancient tales, reworked by Somerset Maugham and others, concerns a Mesopotamian merchant who went down one morning to the market and turned pale when he saw the figure of Death, gibbering and beckoning to him across the square. He fled home and saddled his finest horse, yelling in terror to his chief servant: "I shall flee to Samarra, where Death cannot find me." After his master's hectic departure the servant went down to the same market for provisions. He also saw the figure of Death, which inclined a bony finger in his direction. "I did not mean to frighten your master," said the specter. "I wanted only to remind him that I have an appointment with him this evening—in Samarra."

As I went grinding up the road from Kuwait to southern Iraq last March, in the first few days after a gigantic, mechanized Anglo-American-Australian-Polish army had passed along the same route, I had a similar sense of keeping an unpostponable date. I was watching the closing moments of a war that had begun on August 2, 1990, when the armed forces of Saddam Hussein had smashed in the opposite direction across the Kuwaiti frontier. That conflict had supposedly ended on February 27, 1991, with the official restoration of Kuwaiti sovereignty. But it had smoldered on for more than a dozen years, like a fire raging deep in a bad old mine, and was only now being brought to a conclusion.

I went on a fairly easy day trip, organized by the Muslim Red Crescent, to deliver supplies to the people of Safwan. This is a town inside Iraq, which could claim the faint privilege of being the first center of population liberated from Saddam's control. It lies along the way to the port of Umm Qasr, the harbor by which "the Coalition" aimed to open the hermetic state to the magnificence of the sea and the munificence of humanitarian aid. Dolphins were sporting in the blue waters of Umm Qasr, gaily conscripted as mine detectors, but in Safwan there was a scene of aridity, stagnation and misery. As our relief convoy arrived, with upbeat stencils and slogans on the sides of the trucks, I swiftly realized that it had been fatuous to hope for a greeting of sweets and flowers.

At first, the baked fields around the town appeared inactive if not depopulated. Then a group of children materialized, waving and scampering. Soon, it seemed as if people were rising by magic from the dusty furrows and hillocks. Within moments, the convoy was halted by the sheer press of numbers, and a yelling throng was pressing so close that it prevented the rear doors of the trucks from being opened. After a nasty, undignified scuffle in which some limbs were broken, the Kuwaiti relief workers began to toss the precious cartons out on the heads of the mob, as if supervising frenzy time in some badly run zoo. I don't remember witnessing a more dispiriting scene. The Arab street, whether for or against, is no prettier than any other scene of crowd emotion.

Older people were shoved to the rear, as were the less aggressive children, so one had the chance to talk. On the whole, it was the children who were most enthusiastic about the new arrivals. One of them did an astonishing impression of a helicopter gunship firing down, and then gave an emphatic thumbs-up signal. (Generally, children provide the cheer-up moment in situations like this, so I disliked myself for noticing how many of these had pinched, acne-studded, wolfish faces.) Several of the grown-ups, though, manifested acute resentment and annoyance. "Why do you photograph us like animals?" said one man, shaking with displeasure. "Here—this is how it should be done." And he produced from under his robe an Iraqi government ration book, which, with the help of my translator, I deciphered as a list of his meager entitlements, as a father of four, from the local Baath Party. Gesturing furiously to the winner-take-all grabfest a few hundred yards away, the old boy made it volubly plain that this was not his idea of a fair deal. But he also made it clear that he didn't much like Kuwaitis. A reek of envy was evident: Iraqis have been told for decades that their southern Arab neighbors are rich and fat; fit only to be despoiled of their inherited oil wealth. For this man and others, it was shameful to be the recipient of charity from such a depraved source.

"Boosh, Boosh!" was still the piping chant of the infants and the younger boys, even if some of them did distract the photographers and cameramen by this means, while cunningly letting other kids circle behind to grab wallets and water bottles. A Kuwaiti woman, who hadn't wanted to dismount from the bus, found her privacy and modesty invaded by a small lad who nevertheless proffered a sharp knife. A little earlier, a man named Ajami Saadoun Khilis, who had lost a son and a brother to Saddam, had wept unendingly in the presence of a journalistic colleague of mine, and said: "You just arrived. You're late. What took you so long?" But this, too, was a version of impotence and animosity and humiliation. I found several men—all the women hung back throughout, many of them winding their veils ever closer—who openly praised Saddam Hussein. "He is the only Muslim leader." "He is the only Arab who is a soldier." These were, admittedly, slavish quotations from repetitive regime propaganda, but they were being uttered several days after Saddam's army had dissolved or fled, and they obviously weren't being voiced in the hope of an extra handout.

Another man, wearing a red-and-white headdress, took my sleeve. "Yesterday I saw a British soldier shoot two small children just here on this road." This was a British sector, and there were British military police in the town, so I asked him to tell me more about it. "He shot them with an M-16." I offered to take his complaint to a nearby British officer, even though I know that British forces don't carry M-16s, whereupon he became somewhat evasive and silken. "All right, then," I said. "Forget the officer. Where are the bodies?" "We buried them right away." "And as for the funeral?" "There wasn't time." At this point my companion and interpreter, a vast bear-shaped Palestinian whom I shall call Omar, touched my arm and said, "Come along, Mr. Christopher. These people are all liars."

The Iraqi who had spoken was certainly a liar, and a poor one as well as a mean and low one, but something in me wanted to resist Omar's conclusion. Or perhaps to explain it away. The townspeople of Safwan didn't owe me an explanation. They certainly didn't owe me a welcome, or a friendly pelting with the rose petals they didn't have. They really did live in something like a desert. On previous visits to Iraq I had been embarrassed by the hospitality of those who had much less than I did. On this trip, I felt awkward for the opposite reason. But on this occasion, after all, the soldiers, the relief workers and the reporters outnumbered the population. Should the locals have put on a feast for people who were casually throwing them food? Especially when what they most wanted, and most often mentioned, was water? In the end, even when it takes a vain form or a truculent or sullen shape, pride is an essential part of self-respect. As I departed, a titanic convoy began to roll by. It took forever to pass me, with its massive squadrons of earthmovers, ditchdiggers, tanks and armored cars, feeding one of the longest supply lines in the whole story of warfare and already stretching all the way to the suburbs of Baghdad. By agreement, the soldiers of the Coalition do not fly their national flags on the soil of Iraq. Good. But there was no mistaking their origin, and they roared by the dwarfish mud-brick dwellings without looking to left or right.

I realized that I had seen something faintly similar in my past. It was in Romania in 1989, when the Caligula regime of Nicolae Ceausescu was overthrown by the army and the people. I was in Transylvania at the time, and brought with me some photographs of the late dictator, with his awful wife, Elena, lying riddled with bullets on the floor. Nobody, for the first few days, could believe these pictures to be genuine. It was unthinkable that a man who had occupied the skulls of his people for so long could really be dead. Surely some vampirelike trick had been pulled? And, in the ground-down wasteland of southern Iraq, only the old could remember any time before Saddam. The colonization of the mind still persisted, with trauma right below the surface. It would take more than a few MRE handouts (jambalaya flavor preferred) to dispel this waking and sleeping nightmare.

Just a few months previously, the inhabitants of Safwan had been forced to celebrate not just a 100 percent vote for Saddam Hussein in an official referendum, but a 100 percent turnout as well. What's it like to endure such a sadomasochistic ritual? There are two ways of surviving such a challenge to self-respect. One is the Mafia syndrome, where you play along with the local bosses and learn a shitty way to smile, and one is the Stockholm syndrome, where you make a tiny consolation out of the "security" that the boss can provide. Even the children of Safwan had picked up these elementary lessons.

It had taken me a few days to attain my paltry journalistic ambition of setting foot, however briefly, on the soil of newly liberated Iraq. And the eventual experience had been anticlimactic to say the least. But I gradually came to appreciate that I had been on "liberated" territory the entire time. Twelve years previously, the whole of Kuwait had been appropriated by force as the nineteenth province of an expansionist Iraq. Arab and Muslim countries had fought and invaded each other before, inflicting casualties of the kind that would be called barbaric if imposed by Westerners, but not until 1990 had one Arab state simply abolished the existence of another. The reminders were on every hand. A few miles away from Safwan, the Rumaila oilfields were burning. The field itself straddles the Iraq-Kuwait border, and was one of the prizes coveted by Saddam in 1990. It has over sixteen hundred oil wells, ten of which were ignited by retreating Baathists in the first hours of the recent war and some of which were still ablaze. The heat is so infernally intense that it turns sand into glass around the wellheads, while darkening the sky with choking plumes (like the ghastly, quasi-medieval siege tactics of inflammable oil ditches, set off in Basra and Baghdad by the literally "last ditch" black-shirted diehards of the regime). But in 1991, and in retreat, Saddam had ordered the blowing of more than six hundred wells, and flooded the

Gulf by opening the pipelines. The reprise was only a sputtering, closing version of the original conflagration.

The hysterical vandalism of March 2003 was not comparable with the petro-holocaust of February–March 1991, in point of its scale, but it helped rephrase the whole idea of a war that's "all about oil." Here is a sadistic leader who, if he can't annex the oil for himself, will put it to the torch and toxify the whole regional environment. One experienced the same pungent recollection when responding to the almost-daily air-raid warnings over Kuwait City. At unpredictable intervals, Iraq discharged missiles at its former colony. The generic term for these is "Scuds," though it's not always clear what make or type of weapon is involved. Kuwait City is in theory the best-defended capital in the world when it comes to missile defense, and the new generation of Patriot Interceptors can hit the warhead as well as the projectile, leaving only shards to be analyzed. So we were kept intriguingly in the dark as to whether these were the fabled Al-Summud or Al-Ababil missiles: in other words whether they were missiles with a range already banned by the United Nations or whether the Blix rules didn't actually ban missiles fired at nearby Kuwait. The effect on the ground was somewhat similar: at the first wail of the sirens the people rushed to the shelters and the press corps made a point of looking tough and indifferent. I saw one brief exception to this in late March, when the sirens sounded at midday during a driving sandstorm, and nobody could see anything in the sky. The sound of two high-altitude explosions could be heard almost before the sirens gave the alert, and I did notice a few reporters wrestling with their expensive gas-mask equipment in the streets.

Through the disagreeable atmospheric mixture of pelting sand and burning oil, one could discern no plan or strategy emanating from Baghdad. What was the point of these raids? A single missile hurled from the Iraqi north was meaningless unless it had a chemical or biological payload. And we were continually assured, raid by raid, by the specially trained Czech Chemical Protection Battalion team that was "in country" that the wreckage proved otherwise. The damn things were practically innocuous. The worst night was the last one I was there, when what seemed to be a Chinese-built Silkworm cruise missile managed to get under the radar and to strike a downtown shopping mall. (Iron rule: The one that is successful is the one that doesn't trigger the sirens.) But that effort, too, had less force than a car bomb would have done. The same was true of the shell that whistled over our relief buses as we paused at a roadblock, and banged loudly into the landscape off to our left. It was at the same time vicious and meaningless.

We were parked and pulled over at the time, just near the Mutlaa Ridge. This escarpment is traversable by way of the Mutlaa Pass, a long straight road that connects Kuwait City to southern Iraq. In 1991, it had been the scene of a terrible and disfiguring atrocity committed by the Allied forces. A huge convoy of retreating Iraqis had been straggling back from Kuwait after Saddam Hussein's surrender. It was laden with every refrigerator, television set and item of food or clothing that the late occupiers had been able to carry off with them. This sluggish, crawling monster was caught right out in the open by pilots flying off the deck of the USS *Ranger*. They bombed the front of the convoy to prevent it from going any farther, and they bombed the rear of it to prevent it from retreating. And then they bombed it some more.

The aircrews later breezily described the experience as a "turkey shoot," comparable to strafing the Daytona road during spring break. For hours, while the ship's PA system blasted the *Lone Ranger* theme, they hastened back for fresh loads and roared off to dump the fragmentation bombs onto the helpless thieves below. Then they perforated the remains with armor-piercing and incendiary rounds. The resulting carnage and carrion is imperishably described in *Martyr's Day*, Michael Kelly's book about the "first" Gulf War. (Mike was to be killed on April 3, on the very outskirts of Baghdad International Airport, while riding with the United States Third Infantry Division. He has a monument in the hearts of many friends, Iraqi and American, but that book is his best memorial.)

On the Mutlaa Ridge I came to realize again that I was covering the end of the longest short war, or the shortest long war, that the United States has ever fought. It was in Safwan in 1991, after the eviction of Saddam Hussein from Kuwait, and as the Shia people of southern Iraq were mounting a desperate intifada, that American and Iraqi generals met for an armed truce. The official transcript of the meetings tells the whole story. Lieutenant-General Sultan Hashim Ahmad, representing the Iraqi side, had a request:

We have a point, one point. You might very well know the situation of the roads and bridges and communications. We would like to agree that helicopter flights sometimes are needed to carry some of the officials, government officials or any member that is needed to be transported from one place to another because the roads and bridges are out.

To this clever request, the victorious General Norman Schwarzkopf felt able to give a magnanimous response. As long as none of Saddam's choppers flew over American positions, he replied, there was "absolutely no problem." Hashim Ahmad could scarcely believe his luck, as the transcript shows:

Schwarzkopf: "I want to make sure that's recorded, that military helicopters can fly over Iraq. Not fighters, not bombers."
Hashim Ahmad: "So you mean even helicopters that is [sic] armed in the Iraqi skies can fly, but not the fighters?"
Schwarzkopf: "Yeah, I will instruct our Air Force not to shoot at any helicopters that are flying over the territory of Iraq where we are not located . . ."

And then the rain of horror from the sky, as the Baath Party and its airborne gunships restored order, cleared a space for the special police squads, slaughtered upwards of 50,000 Shia civilians, shelled the holy sites of Najaf and Karbala and recaptured all of the other places whose names have lately become familiar to a mass readership, or in some cases familiar again.

But for the powerless, immiserated population of Safwan, on the day I saw them, it was about twelve years since they'd seen it all before. The big, happy, friendly, gullible Western officers; the fat smiles, the silky grins, the done deal—all déjà vu. Much depended on how smart the second wave would be. A few miles up the road, in the city of Qalat Sukkar, the marines of 2003 arrived with an interpreter and guide named Khuder al-Emiri, who had led a rebellion in the town in 1991 and then escaped with his life. He had been working in Seattle ever since and had volunteered to help with the intervention. He was well liked, and he knew his way around. If there had been more of that kind of intelligent preparation, there could have been much less looting and panic and revenge. As I write this, I am numb with misery about the immolation of the National Museum and the National Library of Baghdad: a disaster to be compared to the Mongol desecrations of antiquity. Yet what if we, and our Iraqi and Kurdish allies, had put an end to the Saddam system in 1991?

I was in Iraqi Kurdistan that summer, and when I look at my old notes and photographs I start to quiver. Here it all is. The victims of chemical bombing in the city of Halabja, some of them with injuries still burning and festering. Villages voided and scorched by Saddam's ethnic cleansing, in a darkened landscape that seems to stretch to hell and back. White-faced refugees and defectors from the south, telling stories of repression that harrow up the soul. But triumphant parades of cars and trucks, with "Boosh, Boosh" chants, and pictures of Bush Senior on the windshield. Exiles returning, at first nervous and tentative and then delighted, from years of enforced emigration. And the odd encounter with laconic British Royal Marines, from 40 Commando, holding the strongpoints on the road. (I have a note of Captain Michael Page and Lieutenant Dominic May in the town of Amadia, telling me that: "Some of Saddam's chaps tried something on our perimeter after nightfall. They rather came off second, though.") Without their presence, and that of other soldiers, the gunships might have finished the annihilation of Kurdistan that year, too.

"Bushistan," they called it then, half in jest and half in tribute. I don't think there's a single picture of Bush Senior in the region these days. And where are you now, Hoshyar my friend, and all the other brave men who more or less carried me across those streams and mountains? Were you by any chance right to be cynical about superpower patronage? Would you have bothered if you thought that Saddam was going to get another dozen years?

Those twelve years were eaten by the locusts. The trunk of the tree of Iraq was allowed to rot, and its branches to wither. And all the time, a huge and voracious maggot lay at the heart of the state. Trade turned into a racket, the market was monopolized by the Mafiosi, the sanctions screwed the poor and fattened the rich, and palaces with gold shit-houses were constructed to mock the slum dwellers and the conscripts. A class of lumpen, uneducated, resentful losers was bred. When the Great Leader wanted to be popular, as on the grand occasion of his last referendum, he declared amnesty for the thieves, rapists and murderers who were his natural constituency. (The political detainees stayed where they were, or are: It will take years for us to find and number all their graves.) To his very last day, the Maggot continued to divide and rule: to pump gangrene and pus into the society, disseminating lies and fear and junky religious propaganda. And there his bastard children were, when the opportunity for hectic destruction and saturnalia presented itself. If it is truly possible to be wise after the event, then I associate myself again with those who believe that the Saddam Hussein regime should have been deposed in 1991. There would have been some severe moments, but Iraq would now be twelve years into the process of nation-building (or rebuilding) and many unlived or blighted lives could have been lived in the risky atmosphere of freedom and self-determination.

I stress the element of risk because it so often seemed to me, before the battle was joined, that many of its critics were demanding the impossible. Assure us of a painless victory, they said, and we might consider lending our support. Assure us, also, of an immaculate conception of the project, unspotted by any previous compromises and betrayals. Assure us above all that oil is an unmentionable bodily secretion, unfit for discussion in polite company. I grew impatient with this. As Frederick Douglass once phrased it, those who want liberty without a fight are asking for the beauty of the ocean without the roar of the storm. (It's been put more tersely more recently: "No Justice—No Peace.") Look back if you care to, and read the wild alarmist predictions that were made. There would be a military quagmire. The Arab street would arise, led by fans of Osama bin Laden, and wreak revenge. Israel would seize the chance to cleanse the West Bank and Gaza of the Palestinians. Turkey would invade northern Iraq. Weapons of chemical and neurological horror—the very ones that Saddam did not possess—would be hurled indiscriminately. Heaps of civilian corpses would rise. Out of an anthology of piffle, I select only Mr. Scott Ritter, veteran of many a "peace" rally, writing in the second week of the Coalition intervention:

> The United States is going to leave with its tail between its legs, defeated. It is a war we cannot win. We do not have the military means to take over Baghdad and for this reason I believe the defeat of the United States in this war is inevitable.

My few days in the vicinity coincided with a memorable sag in the Coalition's campaign and a rapid collapse of morale on the part of the press corps (or to be more precise, a *rise* in the morale of many of them, who had invested themselves and their reputations in a scenario of defeat). As I ventured to say in the essay that opens this collection, I could be fairly immune to this mood because I was politically enlisted with the Iraqi and Kurdish opposition, win or lose. And I still am. And they still haven't won yet, if it comes to that. And they may not win this time, or this round. But they have a chance, and they are fighting a battle for all of us. Just to take one sneer of the nihilistic antiwar faction, about there being no proof of a connection between Saddam Hussein and international gangsterism. Hundreds of the toughest fighters for the regime turned out to be Islamist killers from other nations, hiding behind the human shield of the local population. Even Robert Fisk, the most intransigently anti-Bush reporter of the lot, reported finding some of these tough guys taking refuge in the Palestine Meridien Hotel, home of the international press corps, and lamenting their own failure. Well, who now imagines that this contact between Saddam and the jihad forces began yesterday? The discovery of hundreds of suicide-bomber belts is evidence, as I understand the term. Their discovery in a school—in a *school*—in Baghdad is evidence of evil as well as of intent. As the welcome capture of Abu Abbas, the brave killer of the wheelchair-bound Leon Klinghoffer, also attests—Saddam Hussein was indeed part of an axis of evil. He harbored and trained and financed the scum of the earth, and he preached fantasies of conquest and booty and unholy war, directed at non-Muslims and Muslims alike. The wonder is not that he was eventually taken out, but that he was allowed to go on pumping his gangrene for so long.

The evidence of this decade and more of wasted time was everywhere in Kuwait, and still horribly fresh even after the passage of twelve years. (The Kuwaiti "street" was in no doubt as to which way it wanted this war to go.) Here are the places used as dungeons and execution chambers for fellow Arabs and Muslims. Here is the place where Sheikh al-Ahmed al-Jabir, the most pro-Palestinian man in the country's leadership, was shot down by the Baathist invaders. Here is the citizens' committee which to this day seeks information on the hundreds of Kuwaiti POWs, taken off in blindfolds and never seen again. Here is where the Kuwaiti libraries and museums were gutted. Iraq promised to give compensation and accounting for these and other depredations at the U.N., and never did. It was for all this, and not just because of the morbid ambition to acquire weapons of genocide, that Saddam brought ruinous sanctions on his luckless country.

There was the clinging stench of wickedness left behind from all this, and it was traceable to one nameable individual. Ali Hassan al-Majid, a cousin of Saddam Hussein himself, was placed in charge of the occupation of Kuwait for those seven atrocious months. He had earned this rough promotion with some gusto, having commanded the ethnic cleansing of Iraqi Kurdistan between 1987 and 1988, during which time he boasted openly of using chemical techniques to suppress the population. ("I will kill them all with chemical weapons," he can be heard saying on a notorious tape. "Who is going to say anything? The international community? Fuck them. . . ." Alas, his low opinion of the international community was correct—or at least it was then.) His media nickname—"Chemical Ali"—was entirely too jaunty. He was on every human-rights "Wanted" list in the world, for murder and torture and rape. And in February of 2003 he was appointed to command the southern region of Iraq, and to hold it for Saddam. An easy way to get an expression to change, in the flyblown streets of Safwan, was to mention the name of either man. There was no mistaking the abrupt flash of panic and insecurity that came into the eyes.

Kurdistan, Kuwait . . . and then the pitiless destruction of the independent habitat of the Marsh Arabs near Basra, where the dirty smoke from the immolation of their ancestral territory had been visible from the space shuttle *Endeavor*. Somewhere way up the road ahead from Safwan, there was a rendezvous with this crime family that couldn't any longer be put off. In early April, outside Basra, Ali Hassan al-Majid was (I hope and believe) shredded by a laser-guided missile that was much more selective and scrupulous than the 1991 bombings and strafings had been, and millions of Iraqis and Kurds made a holiday in their hearts. And not very far from the clan hometown of Tikrit is a once-lovely city on the east bank of the river Tigris, containing the tombs of two great imams and a spiral minaret that is one of the region's wonders. In the ninth century, when many Europeans were dressed in skins, it was the shining capital of the Abbasid dynasty. I say "once-lovely" because it has more recently become the site of the most-inspected facility in Iraq, producing at one point an officially admitted four thousand tons of mustard gas, VX, Sarin and other nightmarish chemical agents. Samarra is the name of the town, in case you are curious. It has been waiting for the appointment for a very long time.